LANDLORD/TENANT LAW

by

Margaret C. Jasper, Esq.

Oceana's Legal Almanac Series:
Law for the Layperson

1998
Oceana Publications, Inc.
Dobbs Ferry, N.Y.

Information contained in this work has been obtained by Oceana Publications from sources believed to be reliable. However, neither the Publisher nor its authors guarantee the accuracy or completeness of any information published herein, and neither Oceana nor its authors shall be responsible for any errors, omissions or damages arising from the use of this information. This work is published with the understanding that Oceana and its authors are supplying information, but are not attempting to render legal or other professional services. If such services are required, the assistance of an appropriate professional should be sought.

You may order this or any other Oceana publications by visiting Oceana's Web Site at http://www.oceanalaw.com

Library of Congress Cataloging-in-Publication Data

Jasper, Margaret C.
    Landlord / tenant law / by Margaret C. Jasper.
        p. cm. — (Oceana's legal almanac series. Law for the layperson)
    ISBN 0-379-11249-3 (alk. paper)
    1. Landlord and tenant—United States—Popular works.
  I. Title. II. Series.
  KF590.Z9J37 1998
  346.7304'34—dc21

                                98-45130
                                     CIP

Oceana's Legal Almanac Series: Law for the Layperson
ISSN: 1075-7376

Manufactured in the United States of America on acid-free paper.

To My Husband Chris

**Your love and support
are my motivation and inspiration**

-and-

In memory of my son, Jimmy

ABOUT THE AUTHOR

MARGARET C. JASPER is an attorney engaged in the general practice of law in South Salem, New York, concentrating in the areas of personal injury and entertainment law. Ms. Jasper holds a Juris Doctor degree from Pace University School of Law, White Plains, New York, is a member of the New York and Connecticut bars, and is certified to practice before the United States District Courts for the Southern and Eastern Districts of New York, and the United States Supreme Court.

Ms. Jasper has been appointed to the panel of arbitrators of the American Arbitration Association and the law guardian panel for the Family Court of the State of New York, is a member of the Association of Trial Lawyers of America, and is a New York State licensed real estate broker and member of the Westchester County Board of Realtors, operating as Jasper Real Estate, in South Salem, New York.

Ms. Jasper is the author and general editor of the following legal almanacs: Juvenile Justice and Children's Law; Marriage and Divorce; Estate Planning; The Law of Contracts; The Law of Dispute Resolution; Law for the Small Business Owner; The Law of Personal Injury; Real Estate Law for the Homeowner and Broker; Everyday Legal Forms; Dictionary of Selected Legal Terms; The Law of Medical Malpractice; The Law of Product Liability; The Law of No-Fault Insurance; The Law of Immigration; The Law of Libel and Slander; The Law of Buying and Selling; Elder Law; The Right to Die; AIDS Law; The Law of Obscenity and Pornography; The Law of Child Custody; The Law of Debt Collection; Consumer Rights Law; Bankruptcy Law for the Individual Debtor; Victim's Rights Law; Animal Rights Law; Workers' Compensation Law; Employee Rights in theWorkplace; Probate Law; Environmental Law; Labor Law; The Americans with Disabilities Act; The Law of Capital Punishment; Education Law; and The Law of Violence Against Women.

TABLE OF CONTENTS

INTRODUCTION

Disputes between tenants and their landlords are a common occurrence. Many of these conflicts can be avoided if the parties were more knowledgeable about the landlord-tenant relationship and the attendant rights and responsibilities of each party.

This almanac discusses the landlord-tenant relationship, and sets forth the basic legal rights afforded both the tenant and the landlord under the law, as well as the legal obligations to each other created by virtue of this relationship. The topic of leases and rental agreements, and the manner in which they may alter the rights and responsibilities of the parties, is also discussed. This almanac also explores the circumstances under which the landlord-tenant relationship may end, including abandonment, voluntary termination, and eviction proceedings.

This almanac suggests guidelines for the prospective tenant to follow in searching for suitable rental property, and discusses relevant provisions of the Fair Housing Law and other statutory prohibitions against housing discrimination.

The Appendix provides resource directories, applicable statutes, and other pertinent information and data. The Glossary contains definitions of many of the terms used throughout the almanac.

CHAPTER 1:

THE LANDLORD-TENANT RELATIONSHIP

In General

Landlord-tenant law, as discussed in this legal almanac, refers to the law which governs the rental of residential property. Landlord-tenant law is derived from both statutory law and the common law—i.e., judge-made law. Many states have patterned their landlord-tenant law after the Model Residential Landlord-Tenant Code or the Uniform Residential Landlord And Tenant Act (URLTA).

The Model Landlord-Tenant Act as adopted by the State of Florida is set forth at Appendix 1. The Act gives the reader a comprehensive overview of the typical rights and responsibilities which accompany the landlord-tenant relationship. Nevertheless, because the law may vary from state to state, the reader is advised to check the law of his or her jurisdiction concerning specific issues.

The Landlord

The landlord-tenant relationship is a contractual relationship which is also based in the law of property. In property law, a landlord's interest in the leased property is known as a "freehold" estate. A landlord may be either a fee simple owner of land—i.e. absolute ownership without limitation or condition—or simply a person who has an assignable interest in the property.

The landlord rents or leases the property to the tenant, who thereby obtains the right to the exclusive use and possession of the rental unit during the lease or rental period. The landlord is also referred to as the "lessor" of rental property. The rental property is generally a house, an apartment, a condominium, or room that the tenant rents for the purpose of making his or her home.

In some instances, the landlord or owner hires a property manager to act as an agent on his behalf in managing the property. In that case, the tenant deals directly with the agent instead of the landlord.

The Tenant

A tenant is a person who has the right to use and occupy rental property, pursuant to a rental agreement or lease, provided he or she complies with the terms and conditions of the agreement. The tenant is referred to as the "lessee" of the rental property.

In property law, a tenant's interest in the leased property is known as a "non-freehold" or "leasehold" estate. The tenant, by virtue of his or her agreement with the landlord, acquires an interest in the leased property for a period of time. The specific period of time varies according to the type of rental agreement entered into between the parties. The time period may be indefinite—e.g., a month-to-month tenancy—or for a specified term, e.g. 3 years. During this period of time, the tenant is generally entitled to exclusive possession of the leased property as his or her own.

Under the common law, a tenant is defined as a person who pays consideration to a landlord for the right to occupy property. However, the law applicable to the landlord-tenant relationship only applies to those individuals who are considered tenants under the law of the particular jurisdiction. Examples of some common situations are set forth below. However, the reader is advised to check on the law of his or her own jurisdiction to determine who is considered a tenant and entitled to protection under the applicable law.

Hotel/Motel Residents

In general, hotel and motel residents who meet certain requirements—e.g., they have lived in the hotel or motel for more than 30 days and have paid all of the related charges by the thirtieth day—generally have the same legal rights as tenants. If a hotel resident is considered a tenant as opposed to a mere guest, the hotel manager cannot simply lock the individual out of his or her room, but must take formal legal action through the court to evict the occupant.

In addition, the hotel manager cannot prevent a guest from becoming a tenant by requiring the guest to move before the thirty-day period expires. This is unlawful if the proprietor's purpose is to keep the guest from legally becoming a tenant, and violators are subject to civil penalties and legal fees.

Lodgers

In general, the rights of a lodger renting a room in a private house are the same as those of a tenant. However, in the case of a single lodger in a private house with no other lodgers, his or her rights may be more limited. For example, a lodger may be forced to move following written notice, without a formal eviction proceeding. After the notice period has expired, which is usually the same length of time as the rental payment period, e.g. thirty days, the lodger has no further right to remain in the owner's house and may be removed as a trespasser.

Mobile Home Residents

In general, eviction of mobile home residents is subject to the usual eviction procedures required for tenants, although many jurisdictions have statutes specifically addressing the rights of mobile home and recreational park residents. The reader is again advised to check the law of his or her jurisdiction.

Types of Tenancies

The four basic types of non-freehold estate are the (i) tenancy for years; (ii) periodic tenancy; (iii) tenancy at will; and (iv) tenancy at sufferance.

Tenancy for Years

The tenancy for years—also known as an estate for years—is the most common type of leasehold interest in real property. A tenancy for years is created for a definite, time period, where both the beginning and end of the tenancy term is fixed. The tenancy automatically terminates when the time period ends. Nevertheless, a tenancy for years may end earlier if there is a breach of the lease agreement, e.g., the tenant fails to pay rent.

Periodic Tenancy

A periodic tenancy is one which continues from one period to the next, e.g. month-to-month or week-to-week. The period of the tenancy is generally inferred by how often rent is paid, however, such a tenancy can also be created by express agreement between the parties.

Unlike the tenancy for years, a periodic tenancy has no termination date, but continues indefinitely until one of the parties decides to terminate the agreement, upon advance notice to the other party. Such notice is generally required to be given for the same duration as the period of the tenancy. For example, in a month-to-month tenancy, one month notice of termination is generally required, and for a week-to-week tenancy, one week notice is generally required. However, many states now require a 30-day notice for all such tenancies, regardless of the period involved.

A periodic tenancy may be created following the automatic termination of a tenancy for years. For example, at the end of the fixed lease period, if the tenant does not move out, he or she is known as a "holdover" tenant. The landlord has the option of evicting the tenant or letting the tenant stay. If the landlord opts to let the tenant remain without a lease, a periodic tenancy is created.

Tenancy at Will

A tenancy at will is one which has no fixed duration, and which, under the common law, may be terminated at any time, by either party, without notice. Generally, the tenant is permitted reasonable time to remove his or her property from the premises. Nevertheless, the difference between a tenancy at will and a periodic tenancy has been largely eradicated because many states now statutorily require landlords to give at-will tenants the same right to advance notice as a periodic tenant is given.

Tenancy at Sufferance

A tenancy at sufferance arises when a tenant "holds over"—i.e., fails to vacate the rental property—when the lease expires. The landlord then has the right to either evict the tenant or hold the tenant to another term of the same duration as the expired lease.

If the landlord does not wish to hold the tenant to another lease term, the landlord can treat the holdover tenant as a trespasser. If the tenant continues to pay rent, and the landlord accepts the rental payment, a periodic tenancy may be created as discussed above. Some courts, however, have strictly interpreted such an arrangement as an election by the landlord to hold the tenant over for an entirely new lease term. If the landlord does make such an election, all of the terms and conditions of the previous lease are binding, including the amount of rent.

Privacy Rights

A tenant is entitled to privacy, exclusive possession, and the right to "quiet enjoyment" of the leased property. Thus, a landlord's right of entry is limited. In general, a landlord can enter the rental property: (i) in case of an emergency; (ii) to make necessary repairs or to assess the need for repairs; (iii) to show the property to prospective buyers or tenants; and (iv) upon abandonment of the rental property by the tenant.

In addition, unless there is an emergency, or the tenant has abandoned the premises, the landlord is generally required to give the tenant advance notice—e.g., at least 24 hours—before entering the rental property for any other purpose.

Many states also allow a landlord the right of entry during a tenant's extended absence, in order to maintain the property as needed. However, a landlord may not enter merely to check up on the tenant and the rental property.

Illegal Landlord Actions

A landlord is prohibited from trying to make a tenant abandon the rental property, or from retaliating against a tenant who complains or takes legal action against a landlord. If a landlord takes any illegal actions against the tenant, the landlord may be held liable to the tenant for damages, including legal fees and costs. The following landlord actions have been deemed illegal:

Lockouts

A landlord is prohibited from locking a tenant out of the rental property, e.g., by changing the locks. This is so even if the tenant's rent is in arrears. The landlord's only legal recourse is to begin eviction proceedings.

Utility Shutoffs

A landlord is prohibited from shutting off the utilities to a tenant's rental property for any reason. Further, if the landlord intentionally refuses to pay the utility bills so that the service is terminated, this may also constitute an illegal action.

Removing Tenant Property

A landlord is prohibited from removing a tenant's property from the rental property unless the tenant has abandoned the rental. It would be illegal for the landlord to remove a tenant's property for any other reason.

Renting Property Subject to Condemnation or Housing Code Violations

A landlord is prohibited from renting property which has been condemned, or otherwise rendered uninhabitable due to housing code violations. Housing codes set forth minimally acceptable housing standards, which have long been criticized as being too low. Although housing codes vary according to jurisdiction, these codes generally govern such conditions as plumbing, heat and hot water, electricity, structural integrity, trash removal, and pest control.

Alterations and Modifications to Rental Property

Tenants often choose to alter or modify the rental property, particularly when they have signed a long-term lease. Tenants are entitled to decorate the rental property, however, they sometimes seek to do more than merely re-decorate.

In general, courts have held that a tenant is permitted to alter rental property if "reasonably necessary in order for the tenant to use the leased property in a manner that is reasonable under all the circumstances." For example, it may be reasonable for a tenant to put up a fence around the property if he or she has a dog on the premises. Nevertheless, the landlord still has the right to demand that the tenant restore the property to its original condition prior to the expiration of the lease.

Under some circumstances, the landlord may be able to prevent the tenant from removing a fixture from the rental property. A fixture is an item of personal property—known as "chattel"—which the tenant permanently attaches to the property. The ease of the item's removal and replacement will usually govern whether or not the tenant can remove it when he or she leaves.

For example, the tenant may have the right to remove a ceiling fan because it is relatively easy to detach and replace with a standard light fixture. However, if the tenant installed a decorative sink and vanity in the bathroom, it will most likely have to remain.

If removing the fixture would in some way negatively affect the landlord's interest in the property, or would prevent the property from being restored to its original condition, the courts have generally held that the fixture must remain.

Tenant's Rights Upon Sale or Conversion of Rental Property

Sale

If the landlord sells the rental property prior to the end of the lease term, the tenant maintains the right to live in the rental property until the lease expires, under the same terms and conditions. In addition, the tenant maintains his or her right to have the security deposit refunded at the end of the lease term. Nevertheless, a periodic tenancy can be terminated at anytime upon the required written notice.

Conversion

Over the last ten years, the conversion of rental property into a condominium form of ownership has become commonplace. However, if a landlord wishes to convert his or her rental property into condominiums, approval must generally be obtained from the appropriate governmental authority.

Existing tenants, as well as the general public, are usually entitled to receive notice of the proceedings at various intervals so that they can participate in the process. In particular, written notice of the conversion must be given to existing tenants within a sufficient time period—e.g., six months. Existing tenants may also be entitled to a first option to purchase the property, usually at "insider" prices—i.e., terms that are better than those offered to the general public.

Tenants' Associations

A tenants' association is formed when a group of tenants in a building or complex decide to organize for the purpose of discussing and resolving landlord-tenant problems. Although there are a variety of ways in which a tenants' association can operate, it is common for the tenants to elect a committee. The committee meets regularly to address issues concerning the tenants, and intercede with the landlord on behalf of the tenants.

More organized tenants' associations may also hold forums for tenants to inform them of their rights and responsibilities, and distribute a newsletter to advise the tenants of the committee's activities. Common issues a tenants' association attempts to resolve with a landlord include rent increases, repairs and maintenance, and security issues.

Alternative Dispute Resolution

Legal disputes between landlords and tenants are common, and may arise for a number of reasons, such as a disagreement over a rent increase, or who will take responsibility for certain repairs. Litigation is expensive, and should rarely be the parties' first choice for resolving the dispute. Many leases contain an arbitration clause which provides that the parties arbitrate or mediate disputes arising under the lease. This method of dispute resolution is less expensive and more expeditious than litigation.

A sample lease arbitration clause is set forth at Appendix 2.

CHAPTER 2:

FINDING RENTAL PROPERTY

Setting Guidelines

When searching for rental property, the prospective tenant must consider all related housing costs and make sure that their search is limited to rental property within their housing budget. Some considerations include: (i) the rental amount; (ii) whether utilities are included in the rent; (iii) the amount and availability of funds for a security deposit.

One must also consider the type of rental property they would like to rent—e.g. an apartment or a house,—the desired location, and accessibility to transportation, shopping, schools, etc. It is also important to consider the type and length of rental agreement suitable for the tenant's short and long-term plans, e.g. a tenancy for years or a periodic tenancy, etc.

The Search

Information on rental property is generally located in the classified section of the local newspaper. In addition, some areas carry publications that contain rental listings, which are often published and distributed by local real estate offices. One can also consult public bulletin boards, or drive through the neighborhood looking for rental signs.

In some jurisdictions, there are businesses, known as prepaid rental listing services, which sell lists of available rental units. These businesses are generally subject to government regulation and licensing requirements. If the assistance of a prepaid rental listing service is used, it would be prudent to check out the company's status and reputation before handing over any money.

It is important that the rental information be current and accurate, and that the service guarantee that they will provide a minimum number of listings. The reader is advised to check the law of his or her own jurisdiction concerning the protections afforded prospective tenants when dealing with prepaid rental listing services.

Inspecting the Property

Once a prospective rental property is found, it is important to carefully inspect the condition of the property with the landlord or the property management agent present. Potential problems include: (i) holes or cracks in the walls, ceiling, floor, etc.; (ii) moist areas which may indicate water damage or leaks; (iii) water problems, such as rusty or discolored water, or hot water deficiency; (iv) heating and air conditioning problems; (v) electrical problems, e.g. defective wiring or an insufficient number of outlets, etc.; (vi) damaged furniture if the rental is furnished; (vii) evidence of infestation; (viii) trash removal problems; (ix) environmental problems, e.g., evidence of asbestos which poses serious health hazards if inhaled, or lead paint which can cause lead poisoning and serious health defects in children who ingest chipped paint particles; and (x) the overall cleanliness of the property and its common areas, such as the halls.

When renting a house, it is important to find out who is responsible for maintaining the exterior of the property, e.g., lawn maintenance, snow removal, and general repairs. If the tenant is responsible, this will necessarily increase the overall cost of renting the property.

It would be prudent to make a written inventory of the property—e.g., noting existing damage, and repairs which the landlord agrees to make—which should be dated and signed by all parties. One should also take photographs or videotape the property prior to moving in. This may prove helpful in case there is a dispute about the rental's move-in condition when the tenant seeks reimbursement of the security deposit.

The Rental Application

Most landlords require prospective tenants to complete a rental application. A rental application is a form which requests information concerning an individual's occupation, income, credit worthiness, and references. It is used by the landlord to determine whether or not he wishes to rent to the applicant. Information generally found on a rental application include:

1. Employment history, including the names, addresses, and telephone numbers of present and past employers.

2. Rental history, including the names, addresses, and telephone numbers of your current and past landlords.

3. The names, addresses, and telephone numbers of your personal references.

4. Identifying information, such as driver's license number and social security number.

5. Financial information, including income sources, bank name and address, and bank account numbers.

6. Credit information, including the names and addresses of all creditors and account numbers, and an authorization to obtain a credit report

from a credit reporting agency. The credit report demonstrates whether an individual pays his or her bills on time, whether there are any judgments against the individual, whether the individual has filed bankruptcy, and other financial and credit information during a legally permissible review period—e.g. 7 to 10 years depending on the type of information—which assists the landlord in making a decision to rent.

It is generally illegal for a rental application to request information concerning one's race, color, national origin, ancestry, religion, sex, sexual preference, age, disability status, marital status, or whether there are children under the age of 18 in the household. The subject of unlawful housing discrimination is discussed more fully in Chapter 7 of this almanac.

Nevertheless, it is generally permissible to ask the prospective tenant how many people will be living in the property to prevent overcrowding. State statutes may set occupancy limits, however, as a practical matter, the landlord can require a reasonable standard for the number of people per square feet in the property. Nevertheless, this standard cannot be used as a pretext for refusing to rent to households with children, if the landlord would rent to a household with the identical number of adult occupants.

A landlord is not obligated to tell the prospective tenant the reasons he or she did not qualify for the rental, however, if the decision was based in whole or in part on the individual's credit report, the law generally requires the landlord to so advise the tenant, in writing, and to provide the individual with the name, address and telephone number of the credit reporting agency which rendered the report, and advise the individual that he or she is entitled to a copy of that report, without charge. In addition, upon request, the landlord is obligated to give the prospective tenant a copy of his or her report.

Thus, it is a good idea to obtain a copy of one's own credit report prior to completing the rental application to make sure that it is accurate, to take the opportunity to correct any inaccuracies, and to provide explanations for any negative information appearing in the report. In addition, the landlord may be willing to accept a copy of the applicant's recent credit report instead of incurring the costs to obtain a separate report.

It is generally legal for a landlord to charge a prospective tenant a fee for processing a rental application. The fee is used to offset the costs of investigating the information on the application and obtaining the credit report. However, a fee in excess of the landlord's actual costs is generally not permissible. In addition, the prospective tenant is entitled to know how long the application review process will take.

The Rental Deposit

If the landlord agrees to rent the property to the tenant, but the tenant is unable to take immediate possession of the property, the landlord may request the tenant to place a deposit on the rental—known as a "holding deposit"—for a certain period of time until the tenant pays the necessary security deposit and initial rental payment. The holding deposit is generally nonrefundable, in whole or in part, if the tenant backs out of the deal.

The holding deposit is used to offset the expenses incurred by the landlord in taking the rental property off the market, such as lost rental income. The landlord is then free to rent the property to another. If the holding deposit is given to the landlord at the time the rental application is submitted, but before the applicant is accepted, the landlord is required to return the entire deposit to the applicant if the landlord subsequently decides not to rent to the applicant.

Tenant Selection

Choosing tenants is the most important decision any landlord makes. To do it well, landlords need a reliable system that helps weed out tenants who will pay their rent late, damage the rental property, or cause legal or practical problems later.

A landlord should carefully check all of the information on the prospective tenant's rental application. Before agreeing to rent to the tenant, the landlord should check with previous landlords and other references; verify income, employment and bank account information; and carefully review the prospective tenant's credit report. The credit report is especially important because it will indicate whether a particular person has a history of paying rent or bills late, has gone through bankruptcy, been convicted of a crime or has ever been evicted.

Obtaining Renter's Insurance

Prior to moving into the rental property, the tenant is advised to obtain renter's insurance. Renter's insurance refers to an insurance policy, similar to a homeowner's policy, which insures the tenant for property lost as a result of theft, vandalism, fire or other catastrophe. The policy usually assesses a deductible. In case of a loss, the insurance carrier generally pays the tenant for any losses sustained over and above the deductible.

For example, if personal property valued at $1,000 is stolen from the rental property, and the insurance policy has a deductible of $250, the insurance carrier will reimburse the tenant the sum of $750.

A renter's insurance policy may also include personal liability coverage which protects the tenant from lawsuits filed by others, e.g., a guest injured on the rental property. Renter's insurance pays the other party for their losses, as well as the cost of legal defense.

Although most landlords already have insurance that covers the rental property, this does not necessarily protect the tenant from legal liability. For example, if a tenant negligently causes a fire and destroys the rental property, the landlord may be able to recover his losses from his insurance carrier, however, the insurer may then turn around and seek compensation from the tenant who caused the damage.

Because the price and type of coverage varies among insurance carriers, the tenant is advised to shop around for the best coverage at the best price.

CHAPTER 3:

THE LEASE

In General

Prior to renting, the landlord generally requires the prospective tenant to sign a lease or rental agreement—i.e., the contract that forms the legal basis for the landlord-tenant relationship. The parties to a lease or rental agreement are under a legal duty to deal with each other fairly and in good faith, whether or not the duty is expressed in writing. This means that the parties are to negotiate honestly and in a reasonable manner.

The agreement sets forth the rights and obligations of both parties. Although most agreements are written, oral agreements are legally binding if for a duration less than one year. The problem with oral agreements is that there is no document to look to when a dispute arises over the terms and conditions of the rental.

The primary difference between a lease and a rental agreement is the period of occupancy. A lease sets forth the total amount of time that the lease will be in effect. During this time, the landlord cannot unilaterally change any of the terms and conditions of the rental, such as raise the rent, unless his or her right to do so is set forth in the lease.

This affords a certain measure of protection to the tenant, who has the security of knowing that he or she has a home under a long-term agreement at a set rental amount. Although some leases may contain rental increase provisions, the tenant knows in advance how much of an increase to expect and how often it will be imposed.

Further, the landlord cannot evict a tenant during the lease term, unless for cause, such as non-payment of rent or a violation of a term of the lease which expressly subjects the tenant to eviction. In addition, absent mutual agreement, neither the tenant nor the landlord can end the lease agreement prior to its expiration.

Nevertheless, because the tenant is bound to the lease for its entire period, he or she cannot move, if necessary, without suffering the consequences of breaking the lease. If so, the landlord may be able to recover rent for the balance of the lease period, but usually only until another tenant is found.

A tenant can legally move prior to the expiration of the lease if he or she has good cause to do so. This may occur if the landlord fails to make necessary repairs to the rental property which affects the tenant's ability to enjoy the property—a situation known as "construction eviction."

As discussed in Chapter 1, a periodic tenancy arises when the parties do not wish to commit to a set period of time to be bound to the rental agreement. In that case, they may execute a periodic rental agreement. A periodic rental agreement generally sets forth the length of time which passes between the tenant's obligation to pay the rent—e.g. month-to-month or week-to-week.

Unlike a lease, the periodic rental agreement does not set forth a time period during which the agreement is binding on the parties. Thus, a periodic rental agreement whereby the tenant is obligated to pay rent every month creates a "month-to-month" tenancy, and one which requires the tenant to pay rent every week is known as a "week-to-week" tenancy.

The tenancy is thus extended or renewed for an additional period of time each time the rental payment is made. As long as the rental payments are made, and the landlord does not request the tenant to move out, the tenant is permitted to continue renting the property. The tenancy is automatically renewed at the end of each period unless the tenant or landlord gives written notice that he or she does not want to continue renting the property.

The amount of time which passes between rental payments determines the required notice a tenant must give the landlord if he or she wishes to move out of the rental property. For example, a month-to-month tenant is generally required to give the landlord at least one month's notice before moving.

In addition, the landlord is likewise obligated to give the tenant the same notice if the landlord no longer wants to rent to the tenant, or if the landlord wishes to raise the rental amount or change any other terms of the rental agreement.

The required notice time cannot be less than the period of time between rental payments unless both the landlord and tenant agree, in writing, to a shorter notice period. In addition, many jurisdictions require a minimum notice period of 30 days, regardless of the period involved or whether there has been a contrary agreement between landlord and tenant.

If a periodic rental agreement is undertaken orally,—i.e., without any written terms,—such an agreement is still legally binding on both the landlord and the tenant. However, an oral agreement is more difficult to prove if a dispute should arise concerning the terms of the rental agreement. If the rental is for a period exceeding one year, it must be in writing to be legally binding.

Many landlords use preprinted form leases which often contain a lot of "legalese" that favors the landlord's position. The prospective tenant should read the entire lease before signing, and make sure he or she understand all of its provisions. If the tenant is unsure about any of the terms in the lease, it would be prudent to seek a legal opinion. If the lease contains terms which are inapplicable to the particular rental, make sure that those clauses are stricken.

Some preprinted form leases contain provisions that are not enforceable in a court of law. Examples of illegal terms include but are not limited to: (i) a provision that waives the tenant's rights under the applicable law; (ii) a provision that waives the tenant's right to defend himself in an action by the landlord—e.g., such as an eviction action—or that requires the tenant to pay the landlord's legal fees and costs; (iii) a provision which eliminates or limits the landlord's liability under circumstances where he or she would be legally responsible; or (iv) a provision giving the landlord unlimited access to the rental property without notice. Such clauses should be stricken from the lease.

All leases should include any promises made by the landlord to the tenant which are not already part of the form. Any changes to the printed form must be made in writing and acknowledged by both parties. Any terms which conflict with those changes should be stricken. All changes made to the printed form should be initialed by both parties.

Provisions commonly found in a lease include but are not limited to:

1. The names and addresses of the parties to the lease;

2. The address of the leased property;

3. The amount of rent agreed to be paid under the lease, the due date, and the manner in which it is to be paid, e.g. in person or by mail, etc.;

4. The amount of the required security deposit and the manner in which the deposit will be handled by the landlord;

5. The policy on pets;

6. The manner in which utilities will be paid and who is responsible for paying;

7. A designation of the party responsible for maintaining the property;

8. The manner in which repairs shall be made;

9. Sublease and assignment rights; and

10. The landlord's right of entry provisions.

If the lease presented is one which is drawn up informally by the landlord, it is still binding on the parties. At the very least, a lease should include such basic terms as the landlord's name, address and telephone number; identification of the rental property; rental amount; due date; grace period and late fees; the security deposit amount, and the conditions governing its refund.

Once the lease has been signed by both parties, the tenant should request a signed copy for his or her records and future reference.

A sample residential lease is set forth at Appendix 3.

Rent

Most leases require rent to be paid on a periodic basis as set forth in the lease. For example, a lease may require that rent be paid on a monthly basis by the 15th of each month. Periodic tenancies generally require the rent to be paid at the beginning of each period. For example, a week-to-week tenant may be required to pay rent every Friday, and a month-to-month tenant may be required to pay rent on the 1st of each month.

In order to document that the rent has been paid in case there is a dispute, the tenant should pay by check or money order so they have a receipt. If the tenant pays the rent in cash, he or she must obtain a receipt from the landlord.

A landlord is entitled to charge a late fee if rent is not paid on time, according to the lease. Nevertheless, the late fee must be reasonable in amount. Exorbitant late fees will not likely hold up in a court of law. Many leases contain a "grace period"—i.e., a short time period following the due date during which late fees will not be assessed if the rent is received within that time, e.g. 10 days.

In addition, if the tenant pays his or her rent by check, and the check is dishonored by the bank for any reason, the landlord is entitled to a returned check fee. Again, the amount of the fee must be reasonable, e.g., the penalty charged the landlord by his or her bank as a result of the returned check, plus related costs.

In general, rent cannot be increased during the term of the lease unless the lease expressly provides for such an increase. A landlord can raise the rent for a periodic tenant provided the tenant is given advance written notice within the prescribed period of time, e.g., 30-day notice for a month-to-month tenant and 7-day notice for a week-to-week tenant.

The tenant's duty to pay rent is one of the primary aspects of the landlord-tenant relationship. At common law, a tenant's duty to pay rent continued regardless of whether the landlord breached many or most of the other terms of the agreement. Most jurisdictions have now dispensed with this common-law rule, and hold that a material breach by the landlord of his implied or express obligations relieves the tenant from his or her duty to pay rent until the landlord cures the breach.

For example, if the landlord refuses to make necessary repairs, a tenant generally has the right to withhold the rent and deposit the funds into an escrow account. The tenant may then have the repairs made and deduct the amount of the repairs from the rent.

The tenant's duty to pay rent does not cease if the tenant abandons the property prior to the end of the lease, unless the landlord has violated his or her express or implied duties to make repairs necessary to the enjoyment and habitability of the rental property. In that case, the tenant may legally abandon the rental property under the doctrine of constructive eviction, and the landlord would not be entitled to any additional rent.

Further, if the tenant abandons the rental property, and the landlord takes possession of the property and uses it for his or her own purposes, this implies that the landlord has accepted the tenant's abandonment of the property and also relieves the tenant of the duty to pay any further rent to the landlord.

Security Deposits

A security deposit is a fee, in addition to the first month's rent, which the landlord requires before the tenant moves into the rental property. A landlord is usually limited by the law as to the amount of security deposit he can require the tenant to pay. The purpose of the security deposit is to protect the landlord in case the tenant damages the property during occupancy, or if the tenant moves out without paying the rent. In that case, the landlord is entitled to keep all or part of the security deposit.

Security deposits are generally required to be placed in a bank account, and the tenant must be given information concerning the name of the bank where the funds are being held. Interest earned on the funds generally belongs to the landlord unless there is a written agreement to the contrary, or if the applicable law requires the interest to be turned over to the tenant.

The lease should set forth the amount of security deposit paid, and the circumstances under which the tenant would forfeit all or part of the security deposit. The landlord must give the tenant advance written notice of any increase in the security deposit, if authorized by the lease.

Many leases contain a provision that prohibits the tenant from "committing waste" on the rental property. This basically means that the tenant has the duty to keep the rental property clean, and shall not intentionally or negligently cause damage to the property. This doctrine also requires the tenant to return the rental property to the landlord when the lease expires, in the same condition it was when first occupied, with the exception of reasonable "wear and tear."

If the tenant moves out without owing any rent, and without causing any damage to the rental property above normal wear and tear, he or she is entitled to a refund of the entire security deposit. Many states require landlords to provide the tenant with a detailed list of all deductions taken from a security deposit, whether for unpaid rent or for repairs. The balance of the security deposit, after the deductions are made, is then returned to the tenant, usually within a prescribed period of time, e.g. 2-4 weeks.

The tenant is generally entitled to be present when the landlord inspects the property for damage. This is when the tenant's inventory and pre-rental photos or videotape are most useful. If the landlord tries to hold the tenant liable for any conditions that were in existence prior to the tenant's occupancy, the tenant has written and photographic proof to defend his or her position. If a dispute arises over the security deposit, a tenant may sue the landlord to recover the deposit. Some jurisdictions also award a tenant additional damages and legal fees if they prevail in their lawsuit.

Rent Control and Stabilization Laws

Many jurisdictions have laws which prohibit or limit the amount of rent increase a landlord may assess for rental property—a practice generally known as rent control. Although it is not a new concept, rent control became most prevalent during World War II when the federal government began to regulate the prices of goods, services, and residential rent.

Although federal rent control laws expired in 1950, many rental properties are still under rent-control because state laws permit the tenants to keep them in the family down through the generations. The rent for such properties can only be increased by an amount determined by the government.

Rent stabilization laws were first enacted due to a severe shortage of affordable housing. Rent stabilization laws regulate the amount of rental increases, and govern the manner in which leases may be terminated. One and two-family homes are generally exempt from rent stabilization laws.

Because rent control and rent stabilization laws may vary by state, the reader is advised to check the law of his or her own jurisdiction. For example, some jurisdictions provide that the landlord cannot raise the rent when a new tenant moves into a rent controlled dwelling, while other jurisdictions permit the landlord to increase the rent of a newly vacant apartment to the fair market price.

Subleases

Under certain circumstances, a tenant may desire to sublet his or her property, e.g. the tenant must temporarily relocate due to a job assignment. A sublease is a rental agreement entered into between the original tenant and a new tenant—known as a subtenant—who moves into the rental property while the original lease is still in effect.

The original tenant usually remains solely obligated under the original lease with the landlord, and is still responsible for payment of the rent, unless all three parties agree to relieve the tenant of this obligation. The subtenant becomes responsible for payment of rent to the original tenant, but is not directly obligated to the landlord unless the parties agree.

The sublease between the original tenant and the subtenant should be in writing, contain all essential terms, and be signed by both parties. The rights and responsibilities of the subtenant to the original tenant generally conform to the rights and responsibilities of the original tenant to the landlord. The original tenant cannot give the subtenant any greater rights than he or she has under the original lease. For example, if pets are not allowed in the rental property under the original lease, the sublease cannot permit the subtenant to have a pet on the premises.

In general, a tenant is not allowed to sublet the rental property unless the landlord agrees or the lease allows the tenant to do so. Most leases prohibit subleasing because landlords want to maintain strict control over who occupies the rental property. However, the tenant can seek permission from the landlord to sublet the rental property.

A sample sublease is set forth at Appendix 4.

Assignment of Lease

An assignment of a lease is similar to a sublease in that it is an agreement between an original tenant and a new tenant which gives the new tenant the right to occupy the rental property. However, an assignment is usually sought under circumstances where the original tenant does not intend to return to the rental property, e.g. the tenant purchases a home while the lease is still in effect.

The major distinction between a sublease and an assignment is that the new tenant becomes directly responsible to the landlord as if he were the original tenant. Nevertheless, the original tenant remains obligated to the landlord under the original lease unless all three parties agree that the original tenant will be relieved of his or her obligations under the lease—known as a "novation." In that case, the new tenant becomes solely responsible to the landlord.

For example, if the new tenant reneges on his or her obligation to pay rent, the new tenant is liable to the landlord for the rent even though he or she no longer occupies the rental property. However, if there has been a novation, the new tenant is solely responsible for the unpaid rent, and the landlord can no longer go after the original tenant for payment.

Roommates

Under certain circumstances, a tenant may desire to take in a roommate to help pay the rent and share living costs. This is a typical arrangement for college students living off-campus. A roommate might be either a joint tenant or a subtenant, depending upon the terms of the lease or rental agreement. Taking in a roommate inevitably raises a number of legal questions, which are further discussed below.

In general, the landlord must be notified if the tenant takes in a roommate provided the lease or rental agreement specifically requires the tenant to do so, or if it limits the number of people permitted to occupy the rental property. However, as a practical matter, it is prudent to notify the landlord in any event, so as to avoid a conflict with the landlord which may lead to eviction, particularly where there is a periodic tenancy.

The roommate is not a tenant and thus generally has no legal rights or responsibilities in terms of his or her relationship with the landlord. However, the roommate may take on tenant status if: (i) all parties sign a new lease which includes the roommate as a tenant of the rental property; (ii) the parties orally agree to a landlord-tenant relationship; or (iii) the roommate pays rent directly to the landlord and the landlord accepts the rent, thus creating a contract implied by the conduct of the parties.

However, if the roommate does take on legal status as a tenant, it should be noted that both the roommate and the tenant are now legally obligated to the landlord for the entirety of the rent, not just one-half. Thus, if one of the parties does not pay the rent, the landlord can recover all of the rent from the other party. In addition, both parties would be liable to the landlord for the entire cost of any damages sustained to the property. Of course, both tenants have the right to sue each other to recover monies paid on the other's behalf, however, this may prove a difficult, time-consuming, and costly endeavor.

In any event, whether or not the roommate takes on tenant status, it is important that the roommate and the original tenant put their agreement in writing as to their legal relationship.

Some basic terms which should be included in the agreement include: (i) the amount each party is obligated to pay for their share of rent, utilities and other costs associated with the rental property; (ii) the date and manner in which such payment shall be made; and (iii) the roommate's rights in case the original tenant no longer wants to share the rental property, e.g. notice requirements, etc. Although this agreement is not binding on the landlord, it may become useful if a dispute arises between the tenants.

Shared Utility Meters

Some rental properties use one meter to measure the gas or electrical usage of the entire property, even though there may be more than one tenant in the building, or where the usage includes common areas, such as hallways.

If a shared meter is used, the landlord is obligated to disclose this fact to the tenant prior to signing the lease or rental agreement. A tenant has the right to know what percentage of the total usage he or she will be obligated to pay, and how this percentage will be computed, prior to entering into the agreement.

Spanish Language Rental Agreements

In some states, the law provides that where a spanish-speaking prospective tenant negotiates with a landlord in the Spanish language, the tenant is generally entitled to receive a written translation of the proposed rental agreement before signing. This is so whether or not the tenant requests such a translation. Failure to do so may result in cancellation of the agreement. Nevertheless, if the tenant negotiated the agreement through a qualified interpreter of his or her own choosing, this requirement may be waived.

CHAPTER 4:

LANDLORD LIABILITY

The Warranty of Habitability

At common law, a landlord had no general duty to make repairs and keep the rental property in good working order. In fact, the tenant had the implied duty to make minor repairs to the property, although not required to undertake major repairs. Tenants have made a lot of progress over the last several decades in gaining greater rights in this area.

The warranty of habitability doctrine has now shifted the burden of making repairs from the tenant to the landlord, including minor repairs. This warranty may be either expressed in writing, or implied as an element of the landlord-tenant relationship.

Although some leases still contain a clause which imposes a duty to repair on the tenant, most courts have chosen not to enforce such repair clauses. In addition, clauses which attempt to waive the warranty of habitability have been held invalid as contrary to public policy. A tenant is required to take reasonable care of the rental property, and is generally responsible for damages caused by the tenant, the tenant's guests or the tenant's pets.

Under the warranty of habitability, it is generally required that the landlord ensure, before renting, that the property is habitable—i.e., fit for occupation by humans—and in substantial compliance with building and health codes. In addition, landlords are generally required to maintain the rental property in a habitable condition during the rental period. Minor code violations not affecting habitability, or the failure to undertake minor repairs or cosmetic alterations would not likely violate the implied warranty of habitability.

The sample warranty of habitability clause as codified by New York State is set forth at Appendix 5.

Common defects which may render rental property uninhabitable include but are not limited to:

1. Lack of weather protection, such as broken windows and leaking rooftops;

2. Failure to provide adequate plumbing facilities, including hot and cold running water;

3. Failure to provide an adequate sewage disposal system;

4. Failure to provide adequate heat;

5. Failure to provide adequate lighting;

6. Failure to provide a working stove and refrigerator;

7. Failure to keep the building clean and free from trash and infestation.

If the landlord neglects this responsibility to maintain the rental property, the tenant should put the landlord on written notice of his or her duty to do so. The letter should detail the repairs which need to be made. In addition, the tenant should take photographs of any visible damage. The tenant should keep one copy of the letter and mail the original to the landlord by certified mail with a return receipt to establish that the landlord received the letter.

If after a reasonable period of time the landlord still neglects to make the repairs, there are several courses of action the tenant may take, as discussed below.

Repair and Deduct

Under the "repair and deduct" method, the tenant deducts the amount of money necessary to complete the repairs from his or her rent payment. In order to justify using this remedy, the tenant should only make repairs that breach the warranty of habitability or otherwise threaten the tenant's health and safety.

It is important to keep all repair receipts to justify the amount deducted from the rent. In addition, the tenant should send written notice to the landlord, by certified mail with a return receipt, explaining his or her reasons for deducting the repair money from the rent.

The tenant runs the risk of a lawsuit by the landlord for nonpayment of rent or eviction, and should be prepared to defend his or her right to deduct the repair money from the rent. Nevertheless, the landlord is generally prohibited from taking any action that may be deemed retaliatory, as discussed in Chapter 1 of this almanac.

Rent Withholding

A tenant may choose to withhold all or part of the rent if the landlord refuses to undertake the necessary repairs. Again, the repairs must be serious enough to render the property uninhabitable or threaten the tenant's health and safety. Under this remedy, the rent is not paid until the landlord makes the necessary repairs. The withheld rent should be maintained in an account. The landlord should be advised, in writing, that the rent money is being held in escrow until the repairs are made.

As with the "repair and deduct" remedy above, rent withholding also subjects the tenant to the risk that the landlord will sue for nonpayment of rent or eviction.

Abandonment and Constructive Eviction

A tenant is generally entitled to abandon the rental property without penalty if it is rendered uninhabitable due to the landlord's failure to make necessary repairs. When rental property is uninhabitable, it creates a condition known as "constructive eviction"—i.e., the condition of the property is such that the tenant is unable to enjoy full use and possession and has thus, as a practical matter, been "evicted" from the property. However, to be constructively evicted, the defects must be serious enough to breach the warranty of habitability or otherwise render the rental property unsafe or unhealthy.

If the tenant must abandon the property under these circumstances, he or she is no longer liable for rent under the lease, and is still entitled to a refund of the security deposit. The tenant should send written notice to the landlord, by certified mail with a return receipt, explaining his or her reasons for moving.

Arbitration and Litigation

As set forth in Chapter 1, the landlord and tenant may resort to arbitration or mediation to resolve disputes, including those concerning the condition of the rental property. If alternative dispute resolution fails, the tenant's final option would be to file a lawsuit against the landlord for breach of the warranty of habitability.

If the tenant prevails in a lawsuit, the court may award the tenant any actual damages incurred—such as the cost of alternative lodging—and order the landlord to make the necessary repairs. The tenant may also be able to recover legal fees and costs. Punitive damages may also be assessed if it is found that the landlord's actions were intentional.

A sample Complaint by Tenant for Breach of Warranty of Habitability is set forth at Appendix 6.

The Covenant of Quiet Enjoyment

The covenant of quiet enjoyment is a guarantee to the tenant that he or she is entitled to use the rental property for his or her own enjoyment, without interference by the landlord. If the landlord obstructs or interferes with the tenant's use of the rental property, this would constitute a breach of the covenant.

As discussed above, if the landlord fails to make necessary repairs which threaten the tenant's health and safety and impinge upon the tenant's ability to occupy the premises, this failure may also constitute a breach of the covenant of quiet enjoyment. Nevertheless, the covenant is not breached where the landlord's actions are not serious enough to trigger this clause.

Further, the landlord is generally not responsible for the actions of other tenants unless the landlord either expressly or impliedly authorized any action by a co-tenant which would intrude upon the tenant's quiet enjoyment of the property. For example, the landlord is not responsible because the co-tenants play loud music at all hours of the day and night. The aggrieved tenant may send a copy of the lease agreement to the noisy neighbor.

However, if that doesn't work, the tenant should report the problem to the landlord, in writing. If a number of tenants join in the complaint, the landlord will likely advise the tenant to quiet down or face eviction. If the landlord fails to take any action to reduce the noise after being put on notice, he or she may then be held liable for a breach of the covenant.

A sample Covenant of Quiet Enjoyment of Leased Premises clause is set forth at Appendix 7.

Accidents

A landlord may be liable to the tenant or third parties for injuries caused by dangerous or defective conditions on the rental property. In order to hold the landlord responsible, however, the tenant must be able to prove that the landlord was negligent, and that the landlord's negligence caused an injury. The tenant must be able to show that:

1. The landlord had control over the problem that caused the injury;

2. The accident was foreseeable;

3. Repairing the problem would not have been unreasonably expensive or difficult;

4. A serious injury was the probable consequence of not fixing the problem;

5. The landlord failed to take reasonable steps to avoid the accident;

6. The landlord's failure to repair the problem caused the tenant's accident; and

7. The tenant was genuinely hurt as a result of the landlord's negligence.

For example, if a tenant falls and breaks his ankle on a broken front door step, the landlord will be liable if the tenant can show that:

1. It was the landlord's responsibility to maintain the staircase;

2. An accident of this type was foreseeable;

3. A repair would have been easy or inexpensive;

4. The probable result of a broken step is a serious injury;

5. The landlord failed to take reasonable measures to maintain the steps;

6. The broken step caused his injury; and

7. The victim sustained injuries as a result.

An injured person may file a personal injury lawsuit seeking damages for medical bills, lost earnings, pain and other physical suffering, permanent physical disability and disfigurement, and emotional distress.

Environmental Hazards

The Residential Lead-Based Paint Hazard Reduction Act, commonly known as Title X, was enacted in 1992 to address the serious problem of lead poisoning in children. The Environmental Protection Agency (EPA) is responsible for promulgating the regulations which implement Title X. Title X applies to rental property built before 1978.

Under Title X, prior to signing a lease, the landlord is required to give a prospective tenant a pamphlet prepared by the EPA entitled "Protect Your Family From Lead In Your Home." The landlord and tenant must also both sign an EPA-approved disclosure form demonstrating that the landlord advised the tenants of any known lead paint conditions in the home. This form must be kept on file by the landlord for approximately three years.

If the landlord fails to comply with Title X, he or she faces penalties of up to $10,000 for each violation and treble damages if a tenant is injured by the owner's willful non-compliance.

Additional information on Title X and lead poisoning is available from the National Lead Clearinghouse by telephone at: (800) 424-LEAD, or from the Office of Lead Hazard Control at their internet website: http://www.hud.gov/lea/leahome.html.

The following properties are not covered by Title X:

1. Housing certified as lead-free by an accredited lead inspector;

2. Lofts, efficiencies and studio apartments;

3. Short-term vacation rentals;

4. A single room rented in a residential dwelling;

5. Retirement communities—i.e., housing designed for seniors where one or more tenants is at least 62 years old—unless children are present.

In addition to lead poisoning, landlords may be liable for tenant health problems caused by exposure to other environmental hazards, such as asbestos. The Occupational Safety and Health Administration (OSHA) has issued strict standards for the testing, maintenance and disclosure of asbestos in buildings constructed before 1981. For further information, OSHA may be reached by telephone at: (202) 219-8148 or at their internet website: http://www.osha.gov.

Criminal Activities

Landlords are generally responsible for keeping the rental property safe and secure for tenants and guests—e.g., making sure that doors and windows have proper locks and common areas are well-lit, etc. Most states hold landlords legally responsible to some degree in protecting their tenants from burglars and other criminals, as well as from the criminal actions of co-tenants and employees.

The failure to make a reasonable assessment of the crime potential of the area, and follow up with security measures designed to eliminate or reduce the threat of safety, may subject the landlord to a greater degree of legal liability if a tenant is injured as a result of the landlord's negligence.

Landlords must also be vigilant about tenant crime. For example, the landlord may be held legally responsible for tenants who deal drugs from their apartments, particularly if it can be shown that the landlord was aware of the situation and failed to take any action against the tenant. For this reason, landlords must be particularly careful during the tenant screening process, be aware of activities taking place on the rental property, and take swift action if a problem arises.

Landlords should also be careful when hiring employees, such as a superintendent or building manager, because such employees generally have access to the individual rentals. A thorough background check should be undertaken prior to hiring. If a building employee causes injury or property loss to a tenant, the landlord will generally be held liable under the legal doctrine of "respondeat superior," which states that the employer is liable for the acts of the employees.

CHAPTER 5:

MOVING OUT OF THE RENTAL PROPERTY

In General

A tenant who plans to move must determine his or her legal rights to terminate the tenancy according to the type of agreement entered into with the landlord. If the tenant has signed a valid lease for a set period of time, the tenant cannot move before the expiration of the lease term, unless the landlord agrees to break the lease. In the case of a periodic tenancy, neither the landlord nor the tenant are bound by the rental agreement to any set term. Therefore, upon the required advance notice, either party is entitled to end the tenancy.

Expiration of Lease Term

A lease expires automatically when the set term ends, at which time the tenant must vacate the premises. Tenants who wish to renew their lease and extend the term of their tenancy should do so within a reasonable period of time prior to its expiration. Absent a lease provision to the contrary, the landlord is not entitled to notice because the lease expiration date already puts the landlord on notice that the tenant will be vacating the premises on or before a certain date.

A tenant who does not vacate the rental property on or before the lease expiration date—known as a "holdover" tenant—automatically becomes a periodic tenant if a new lease is not signed and the landlord continues to accept rent. However, if the landlord refuses to accept rent from the holdover tenant, the landlord can begin eviction proceedings, without notice, as set forth in Chapter 6.

Prior to moving, the tenant should request the landlord to inspect the rental property in his or her presence so that any disputes concerning the condition of the property can be addressed and resolved. If the landlord and tenant agree that the rental property is in the same condition upon departure as it was when the tenant arrived, excluding normal wear and tear, the tenant is entitled to a refund of the entire security deposit. If, however, the landlord and tenant agree that there are items in need of repair, the landlord is entitled to deduct the cost of such repairs from the tenant's security deposit.

If a tenant moves out of rental property before the lease term expires, he or she is still liable to the landlord for payment of rent until the expiration date. Nevertheless, the landlord is generally required to make reasonable efforts to rent the property. In that case, the tenant would only be liable for the time the property remained unoccupied. In addition, if the landlord does not attempt to re-rent the property, the tenant may be relieved of his or her obligation to pay some or all of the rent owed.

The Periodic Tenancy

A periodic rental agreement does not contain a set term as does a lease. Therefore, to end a periodic rental agreement, the tenant need only serve the required advance notice upon the landlord. The rental agreement may set forth the required notice period. In general, however, advance notice of termination is 30 days for a month-to-month tenancy, and 7 days for a week-to-week tenancy. Because some jurisdictions may have more stringent notice requirements, the reader is advised to check the law of his or her own jurisdiction.

The tenant should mail the notice to the landlord by certified mail with a return receipt so that there is no dispute over when the landlord received the tenant's notice. The notice should state when the tenant intends to vacate the premises.

A sample Notice to Landlord of Tenant's Intention to Vacate Leased Premises is set forth at Appendix 8.

Abandonment of Rental Property

If a tenant fails to pay rent, and then leaves the rental property without any notice, prior to the expiration of the lease term, the tenant is considered to have "abandoned" the property. If the landlord suspects that the rental property has been abandoned, he or she is entitled to enter the property, remove any belongings left behind by the tenant, and re-take possession of the property.

The landlord is generally required to store any removed property belonging to the tenant for a reasonable period of time. A notice should be mailed to the tenant at the rental property address so that the Post Office can send it to the tenant's forwarding address, if any. The notice should advise the tenant that the abandoned property will be sold if not claimed within a certain time period.

If the property is not claimed after a reasonable period of time, the landlord may sell the property and apply the proceeds to back rent. Nevertheless, prior to any sale, the landlord should make certain that the tenant did, in fact, abandon the property, or risk having to compensate the tenant at some later date.

Under certain circumstances, a tenant is justified in breaking the lease or abandoning the rental property, including but not limited to situations where: (i) the property becomes uninhabitable such that it threatens the health and safety of the tenant; (ii) the property is destroyed, e.g. by fire or other disaster; or (iii) the landlord breaches a material term of the lease.

CHAPTER 6:

TERMINATIONS AND EVICTIONS

In General

If a landlord wants to remove a tenant, there are legally prescribed methods which must be followed. The landlord is not entitled to physically remove the tenant and his or her belongings from the rental property, nor can the landlord make living conditions uninhabitable to try and force the tenant to leave. These types of tactics—generally known as "self-help" measures—are illegal and may result in the landlord having to pay the tenant's damages.

The landlord is usually required to serve the tenant with some type of written notice before terminating the tenancy. Where there is a valid lease, the landlord cannot terminate the tenancy unless he or she has just cause to do so, e.g., the tenant violates a term contained in the lease. If the landlord believes that he or she has just cause to evict the tenant, a three-day notice will be served, as further described below.

In the case of a periodic tenancy, because the rental agreement contains no fixed term, in addition to serving a three-day notice for cause, the landlord is entitled to terminate the tenancy at any time, for no cause whatsoever, provided the landlord serves the tenant with the required advance notice of termination.

As discussed below, the termination notice is generally known as a thirty-day notice, since most periodic tenancies are month-to-month agreements. A week-to-week tenancy may only require a seven-day notice. However, some jurisdictions may have more stringent notice requirements, therefore, the reader is advised to check the law of his or her own jurisdiction.

The Three-Day Notice

A landlord may serve a three-day eviction notice on a tenant who breaches his or her lease or rental agreement. The three-day notice must be properly served upon the tenant—i.e., served in a manner prescribed by the applicable law—to be effective. Proper service must be made upon the tenant to be reasonably certain that the tenant is aware of the action being taken, and has an opportunity to respond.

In general, the landlord or someone acting on behalf of the landlord may serve the notice provided he or she is over the age of 18. There are three principal ways service is generally undertaken:

1. Personal Service—Personal service is accomplished by handing the notice to the tenant. If the tenant refuses to take the notice, the server is authorized to leave the notice in the tenant's immediate vicinity after advising the tenant that the notice is being served upon him or her.

2. Substituted Service—Substituted service is accomplished by leaving the notice with "a person of suitable age and discretion" at the tenant's home or place of business. Service is completed when a copy of the notice is also mailed to the tenant at his or her home address.

3. Nail and Mail—Nail and mail service is accomplished by affixing a copy of the notice to the front door of the rental property. Service is completed when a copy of the notice is also mailed to the tenant at his or her home address. This method is generally used when personal service and substituted service have been unsuccessful.

The most common reasons for eviction include but are not limited to: (i) non-payment of rent; (ii) creating a nuisance; (iii) committing illegal activities on the rental property; and (iv) damaging the rental property. The three-day notice must advise the tenant of the reason he or she is being evicted. If the three-day notice is due to non-payment of rent, the landlord must specify the amount of rent due.

Three-day notices generally give the tenant the option of either curing the problem or moving. If the notice was served because of non-payment of rent, the tenant may remain in the rental property if he or she pays the arrears within the three-day period. If the rent is not paid until after the three-day period expires, the landlord has the option of either accepting the late payment, or evicting the tenant and demanding a judgment for any past due rent.

If the three-day notice was served for a reason other than non-payment of rent, the notice usually states whether the problem can be corrected. If the tenant wishes to remain in the rental property, he or she must correct the violation within the three-day period, and should notify the landlord immediately that the violation has been rectified.

If the violation is one which cannot be corrected—e.g., the tenant is being evicted because he or she caused substantial damage to the property—the tenant has no recourse but to leave the premises when the three-day period has expired.

Although the notice may be called a "three-day" notice, it does not necessarily expire at the end of the third day. The first day of the "three-day" period begins the day following the day the tenant was served with the notice, and cannot end on a Saturday or Sunday. For example, if the three-day notice was served upon the tenant on Wednesday, the first day of the three-day period is Thursday and the actual third day would fall on a Saturday. Thus, the tenant has an additional two days, until Monday of the following week, to correct the violation.

Nevertheless, the landlord is prohibited by law from evicting a tenant unlawfully. As discussed in Chapter 1, this may occur if the landlord is acting in retaliation against the tenant because of some prior complaint the tenant may have made against the landlord. If the tenant suspects the landlord's eviction is unlawful or otherwise defensible, he or she is advised to seek legal counsel.

A sample Three-Day Notice to Tenant to Vacate Leased Premises Due to Non-payment of Rent is set forth at Appendix 9.

The Thirty-Day Notice

In addition to termination for cause, a landlord can terminate a periodic tenancy at any time by merely giving the tenant the required notice. In general, notice is usually required 30 days in advance for a month-to-month tenancy, unless the rental agreement provides for a longer or shorter notice period. A thirty-day notice may be served by any of the methods described above, or by certified or registered mail.

If, however, the tenant has violated the rental agreement—e.g. failed to pay rent—the landlord is only required to give the tenant the three-day notice as discussed above.

The thirty-day notice does not have to state the landlord's reasons for ending the tenancy, unless a local law requires it. For example, some rent control and subsidized housing regulations require "just cause" for eviction, even for periodic tenancies.

A periodic tenant who receives a thirty-day notice generally has no legal right to stay in the rental property beyond the thirty days. If this would pose a grave hardship, the tenant should immediately try and work out some alternative arrangement with the landlord. If the landlord grants an extension, it should be in writing. If the tenant fails to move after the thirty-day period expires, the landlord has the right to begin an eviction proceeding against the holdover tenant.

The Eviction Lawsuit

If a tenant does not move after the three-day notice for cause expires—or in the case of a periodic tenant, after the expiration of 30 days without cause—the landlord must bring an eviction lawsuit against the tenant, also known as an "unlawful detainer" lawsuit, in order to remove the tenant from the rental property.

The landlord, as plaintiff, must file a complaint against the tenant, as defendant, in the appropriate court. Eviction proceedings—also known as summary proceedings—are intended to move swiftly through an otherwise slow-moving judicial system. The tenant's time to respond to the landlord's complaint is relatively short, e.g. 5 days.

In the response, the tenant should set forth any defenses he or she may have, e.g., that the eviction is unlawful because it is in retaliation for some action taken against the landlord, or that the rental property violates the implied warranty of habitability and the tenant was authorized to withhold the rent, etc. It is imperative that the tenant respond to the landlord's complaint because failure to do so may result in a default judgment.

After the tenant's answer has been served and filed, the court generally holds a hearing at which time both the landlord and tenant present their evidence and make their arguments. If the court rules for the tenant, the landlord may be held liable for the tenant's damages, including legal fees and costs. In addition, the tenant would be entitled to remain in the rental property.

If the landlord prevails, the judge issues an order that the tenant be removed from the rental property. This order is generally carried out by the sheriff. The tenant can voluntarily leave the premises at anytime between issuance of the order and its implementation by the sheriff. The sheriff is authorized to physically remove the tenant and to seize any items left in the rental property. Once the sheriff has executed the order, the landlord is entitled to take possession of the rental property. The judge may also award the landlord a judgment for unpaid rent, legal fees and costs.

CHAPTER 7:

HOUSING DISCRIMINATION

In General

Federal, state and local fair housing laws provide protection to prospective tenants against housing discrimination. These laws set forth the illegal reasons to refuse to rent to a tenant. Landlords are still free to choose among prospective tenants, as long as their decisions comply with these laws and are based on legitimate business criteria.

For example, a landlord is entitled to reject an individual who has a bad credit history, insufficient income to pay the rent, or past negative behavior—such as having caused property damage—that makes the person a bad risk. A valid occupancy policy limiting the number of people per rental, based on health and safety concerns, or on the rental property's plumbing or electrical capacities, may also be a legal basis for refusing tenants.

It is illegal for a landlord to refuse to rent to a tenant on the basis of group characteristics specified by law that are not closely related to the business needs of the landlord. In general, discrimination based on the following factors have been deemed illegal under various federal and state statutes: (i) race, (ii) color, (iii) religion, (iv) sex, (v) marital status, (vi) national origin, (vii) ancestry, (viii) familial status, (ix) mental disability, (x) physical disability, and (xi) sexual orientation.

Further, it is illegal for landlords to discriminate against families with children, although specially designated senior citizen housing may set a minimum age requirement for all occupants. The reader is advised to check the law of his or her own jurisdiction concerning the categories of discrimination that are deemed illegal, as some states may afford greater coverage than others.

Owner-occupied, single-family homeowners who rent out a single room in the home to a lodger, where there are no other lodgers living in the household, are not subject to some of the restrictions on illegal discrimination. Nevertheless, the owner cannot make oral or written statements, or use notices or advertisements which indicate any preference, limitation, or discrimination practice. However, a person in a single-family home seeking a roommate may express a gender preference if there will be common living areas.

Remedies

As further discussed below, a victim of discrimination may file a housing discrimination complaint with the United States Department of Housing and Urban Development (HUD). HUD will investigate the complaint and take action if warranted. If the discrimination is a violation of a state fair housing law, the tenant may wish to file a complaint with the state agency in charge of enforcing the law. Instead of filing a complaint with HUD or a state agency, the complainant may choose to file a lawsuit directly in federal or state court.

An individual who is subjected to illegal housing discrimination is generally entitled to recover damages, which may include: (i) monetary compensation for actual damages, including reimbursement for expenses incurred in seeking alternative housing; (ii) the right to obtain the desired housing; (iii) any other damages suffered which are provable; and (iv) legal fees and costs.

Victims of housing discrimination may obtain further information and assistance by contacting HUD. In addition, many jurisdictions have their own local fair housing organizations and consumer protection agencies which can be a source of further information. Legal aid organizations may also provide free advice and/or representation to persons who qualify for services. There are also private attorneys who specialize in housing discrimination litigation.

As further discussed below, HUD enforces the federal Fair Housing Act, which prohibits discrimination based on race, color, national origin, religion, sex, family status, or disability. Nevertheless, the Federal Fair Housing Act provisions do not replace any state or local laws which provide greater requirements.

A directory of HUD Fair Housing Offices is set forth at Appendix 10.

The Federal Fair Housing Act

The Fair Housing Act prohibits housing discrimination based on one's race, color, national origin, religion, sex, family status, or disability, and provides that no one may take any of the following actions if based on these factors:

1. Refuse to rent or sell housing;

2. Refuse to negotiate for housing;

3. Make housing unavailable;

4. Deny a dwelling;

5. Set different terms, conditions or privileges for sale or rental of a dwelling;

6. Provide different housing services or facilities;

7. Falsely deny that housing is available for inspection, sale, or rental;

8. For profit, persuade owners to sell or rent, an activity known as blockbusting; or

9. Deny anyone access to, or membership in, a facility or service related to the sale or rental of housing.

In addition, it is illegal to (i) threaten, coerce, intimidate or interfere with anyone who is exercising a fair housing right, or assisting others who exercise that right; and to (ii) advertise or make any statement that indicates a limitation or preference based on race, color, national origin, religion, sex, familial status, or handicap.

Selected provisions of the Fair Housing Act are set forth at Appendix 11.

Additional Provisions Related to Disabled Persons

If an individual, or someone associated with the individual, has a physical or mental disability that substantially limits one or more major life activities, and has a record of such a disability or is regarded as having such a disability, a landlord may not:

1. Refuse to let the tenant make reasonable modifications to the dwelling or common use areas, at the tenant's own expense, if necessary, for the disabled person to use the housing.

2. Refuse to make reasonable accommodations in rules, policies, practices or services if necessary for the disabled person to use the housing.

Nevertheless, housing need not be made available to a person who is a direct threat to the health or safety of others or who currently uses illegal drugs.

For buildings that were ready for first occupancy after March 13, 1991, and which have an elevator and four or more units, the following provisions apply:

1. The public and common areas must be accessible to persons with disabilities;

2. The doors and hallways must be wide enough for wheelchairs;

3, All units must have (i) an accessible route into and through the unit; (ii) accessible light switches, electrical outlets, thermostats and other environmental controls; (iii) reinforced bathroom walls to allow later installation of grab bars; and (iv) kitchens and bathrooms that can be used by people in wheelchairs. For those buildings that do not have an elevator, the aforementioned standards apply to the ground floor units.

The landlord is required by law to permit a disabled tenant to make reasonable modifications to the rental property to the extent necessary for the tenant to have what is known as "full enjoyment of the premises." The tenant, however, is generally required to pay the costs for any such modifications. Further, the tenant may be required to restore the rental property to its prior condition when the tenant moves out.

Federal Fair Housing Law Exemptions

Under certain circumstances, the following properties may be exempt from the federal law:

Small/Owner-Occupied Properties

This exemption generally applies to residential property that is owned by "mom and pop" landlords—e.g. individuals who own three single family homes or less at any one time—or owner-occupied buildings that have four units or less where the owner resides in one of the units.

Religious Organizations and Private Clubs

A restriction on the sale or rental of property owned by religious organizations and private clubs may be limited to their members, if they meet the federal guidelines. Anyone who seeks to use this exception to the Fair Housing Law should confirm it with competent legal counsel first, as an error in interpretation could prove costly.

Senior Citizen Housing

A landlord can only discriminate against tenants with children concerning housing if: (i) the HUD Secretary has determined that it is specifically designed for and occupied by elderly persons under a Federal, State or local government program; or (ii) it is occupied solely by persons who are 62 or older; or (iii) it houses at least one person who is 55 or older in at least 80 percent of the occupied units, and adheres to a policy that demonstrates an intent to house persons who are 55 or older.

Nevertheless, property owners who are otherwise exempt from the law must still comply with the prohibitions against discrimination in advertising. As it relates to senior citizen housing, the advertising is permitted to state that the building does not allow children, or that it is an "Over 55" building, however, the advertising cannot discriminate against other protected classes under the Fair Housing Law.

Remedies Under the Fair Housing Act

Filing a HUD Complaint

A tenant who thinks that a landlord has broken a federal fair housing law can file a complaint with Hud's Office of Fair Housing and Equal Opportunity. Complaints must be filed with HUD within one year of the alleged discriminatory act.

If HUD determines that the tenant's State or local agency has the same fair housing powers as HUD, HUD will refer the complaint to that agency for investigation and notify the complainant of the referral. That agency must begin work on the complaint within 30 days or HUD may reclaim the complaint.

A complaint may be filed with HUD by phone, mail or on-line as follows:

> Department of Housing and Urban Development
> Office of Fair Housing and Equal Opportunity
> 451 Seventh Street S.W.
> Washington, DC 20410-2000
> Telephone: 1-800-669-9777
> (TTY): 1-800-927-9275.
> Website: http://www.fairhousing.org/

When filing a complaint with HUD, be prepared to give the following information:

1. Your name and address;

2. The name and address of the person your complaint is about;

3. The address of the house or apartment you were trying to rent or buy;

4. The date when the incident occurred; and

5. A short description of the incident.

HUD will notify the complainant when it receives the complaint. HUD will also notify the alleged violator—called the "respondent"—and permit that person to submit an answer to the complaint. HUD will then investigate the complaint and determine whether there is reasonable cause to believe the Fair Housing Act has been violated.

HUD will then normally appoint a mediator to negotiate with the landlord and reach a settlement, also known as a "conciliation." A conciliation agreement must protect both the individual complainant and the public interest. If an agreement is reached, HUD will take no further action on the complaint unless HUD has reasonable cause to believe that the conciliation agreement is breached. In that case, HUD will generally recommend that the Attorney General file suit.

If HUD is unable to negotiate a settlement, an administrative hearing may be held to determine whether discrimination has occurred. If the case does go to an administrative hearing, HUD attorneys will litigate the case on the complainant's behalf. An Administrative Law Judge (ALJ) will consider evidence from the complainant and the respondent. If the ALJ decides that discrimination occurred, the respondent can be ordered:

1. To pay compensation for actual damages, including humiliation, pain and suffering;

2. To provide injunctive or other equitable relief, for example, to make the housing available;

3. To pay the Federal Government a civil penalty to vindicate the public interest. The maximum penalties are $10,000 for a first violation and $50,000 for a third violation within seven years.

4. To pay reasonable attorney's fees and costs.

If there is noncompliance with the ALJ's order, HUD may seek temporary relief, enforcement of the order or a restraining order in a United States Court of Appeals. In addition, the Attorney General may file a suit in a Federal District Court if there is reasonable cause to believe a pattern or practice of housing discrimination is occurring.

Federal District Court

If the complainant or respondent chooses to have the case decided in Federal District Court instead of at an administrative hearing, the Attorney General will file a suit and litigate it on the complainant's behalf. Like the ALJ, the District Court can order relief, and award actual damages, attorney's fees and costs. In addition, the court can award punitive damages.

Individual Civil Lawsuit

The complainant is also entitled to file their own individual civil lawsuit in Federal District Court or State Court within two years of an alleged violation. This is so even if the complainant already filed a complaint with HUD, provided he or she has not signed a conciliation agreement, or an ALJ has not started an administrative hearing. If the tenant prevails, the court may award actual and punitive damages and attorney's fees and costs.

APPENDICES

APPENDIX 1:

MODEL LANDLORD TENANT ACT—STATE OF FLORIDA

83.40 Short title.—

This part shall be known as the "Florida Residential Landlord and Tenant Act."

83.41 Application.—

This part applies to the rental of a dwelling unit.

83.42 Exclusions from application of part.—

This part does not apply to:

(1) Residency or detention in a facility, whether public or private, when residence or detention is incidental to the provision of medical, geriatric, educational, counseling, religious, or similar services.

(2) Occupancy under a contract of sale of a dwelling unit or the property of which it is a part.

(3) Transient occupancy in a hotel, condominium, motel, rooming-house, or similar public lodging, or transient occupancy in a mobile home park.

(4) Occupancy by a holder of a proprietary lease in a cooperative apartment.

(5) Occupancy by an owner of a condominium unit.

83.43 Definitions.—

As used in this part, the following words and terms shall have the following meanings unless some other meaning is plainly indicated:

(1) "Building, housing, and health codes" means any law, ordinance, or governmental regulation concerning health, safety, sanitation or fitness for habitation, or the construction, maintenance, operation, occupancy, use, or appearance, of any dwelling unit.

(2) "Dwelling unit" means:

(a) A structure or part of a structure that is rented for use as a home, residence, or sleeping place by one person or by two or more persons who maintain a common household.

(b) A mobile home rented by a tenant.

(c) A structure or part of a structure that is furnished, with or without rent, as an incident of employment for use as a home, residence, or sleeping place by one or more persons.

(3) "Landlord" means the owner or lessor of a dwelling unit.

(4) "Tenant" means any person entitled to occupy a dwelling unit under a rental agreement.

(5) "Premises" means a dwelling unit and the structure of which it is a part and a mobile home lot and the appurtenant facilities and grounds, areas, facilities, and property held out for the use of tenants generally.

(6) "Rent" means the periodic payments due the landlord from the tenant for occupancy under a rental agreement and any other payments due the landlord from the tenant as may be designated as rent in a written rental agreement.

(7) "Rental agreement" means any written agreement, or oral agreement if for less duration than 1 year, providing for use and occupancy of premises.

(8) "Good faith" means honesty in fact in the conduct or transaction concerned.

(9) "Advance rent" means moneys paid to the landlord to be applied to future rent payment periods, but does not include rent paid in advance for a current rent payment period.

(10) "Transient occupancy" means occupancy when it is the intention of the parties that the occupancy will be temporary.

(11) "Deposit money" means any money held by the landlord on behalf of the tenant, including, but not limited to, damage deposits, security deposits, advance rent deposit, pet deposit, or any contractual deposit agreed to between landlord and tenant either in writing or orally.

(12) "Security deposits" means any moneys held by the landlord as security for the performance of the rental agreement, including, but not limited to, monetary damage to the landlord caused by the tenant's breach of lease prior to the expiration thereof.

(13) "Legal holiday" means holidays observed by the clerk of the court.

83.44 Obligation of good faith.—

Every rental agreement or duty within this part imposes an obligation of good faith in its performance or enforcement.

83.45 Unconscionable rental agreement or provision.—

(1) If the court as a matter of law finds a rental agreement or any provision of a rental agreement to have been unconscionable at the time it was made, the court may refuse to enforce the rental agreement, enforce the remainder of the rental agreement without the unconscionable provision, or so limit the application of any unconscionable provision as to avoid any unconscionable result.

(2) When it is claimed or appears to the court that the rental agreement or any provision thereof may be unconscionable, the parties shall be afforded a reasonable opportunity to present evidence as to meaning, relationship of the parties, purpose, and effect to aid the court in making the determination.

83.46 Rent; duration of tenancies.—

(1) Unless otherwise agreed, rent is payable without demand or notice; periodic rent is payable at the beginning of each rent payment period; and rent is uniformly apportionable from day to day.

(2) If the rental agreement contains no provision as to duration of the tenancy, the duration is determined by the periods for which the rent is payable. If the rent is payable weekly, then the tenancy is from week to week; if payable monthly, tenancy is from month to month; if payable quarterly, tenancy is from quarter to quarter; if payable yearly, tenancy is from year to year.

(3) If the dwelling unit is furnished without rent as an incident of employment and there is no agreement as to the duration of the tenancy, the duration is determined by the periods for which wages are payable. If wages are payable weekly or more frequently, then the tenancy is from week to week; and if wages are payable monthly or no wages are payable, then the tenancy is from month to month. In the event that the employee ceases employment, the employer shall be entitled to rent for the period from the day after the employee ceases employment until the day that the dwelling unit is vacated at a rate equivalent to the rate charged for similarly situated residences in the area. This subsection shall not apply to an employee or a resident manager of an apartment house or an apartment complex when there is a written agreement to the contrary.

83.47 Prohibited provisions in rental agreements.—

(1) A provision in a rental agreement is void and unenforceable to the extent that it:

(a) Purports to waive or preclude the rights, remedies, or requirements set forth in this part.

(b) Purports to limit or preclude any liability of the landlord to the tenant or of the tenant to the landlord, arising under law.

(2) If such a void and unenforceable provision is included in a rental agreement entered into, extended, or renewed after the effective date of this part and either party suffers actual damages as a result of the inclusion, the aggrieved party may recover those damages sustained after the effective date of this part.

83.48 Attorney's fees.—

In any civil action brought to enforce the provisions of the rental agreement or this part, the party in whose favor a judgment or decree has been rendered may recover reasonable court costs, including attorney's fees, from the nonprevailing party.

83.49 Deposit money or advance rent; duty of landlord and tenant.—

(1) Whenever money is deposited or advanced by a tenant on a rental agreement as security for performance of the rental agreement or as advance rent for other than the next immediate rental period, the landlord or the landlord's agent shall either:

(a) Hold the total amount of such money in a separate non-interest-bearing account in a Florida banking institution for the benefit of the tenant or tenants. The landlord shall not commingle such moneys with any other funds of the landlord or hypothecate, pledge, or in any other way make use of such moneys until such moneys are actually due the landlord;

(b) Hold the total amount of such money in a separate interest-bearing account in a Florida banking institution for the benefit of the tenant or tenants, in which case the tenant shall receive and collect interest in an amount of at least 75 percent of the annualized average interest rate payable on such account or interest at the rate of 5 percent per year, simple interest, whichever the landlord elects. The landlord shall not commingle such moneys with any other funds of the landlord or hypothecate, pledge, or in any other way make use of such moneys until such moneys are actually due the landlord; or

(c) Post a surety bond, executed by the landlord as principal and a surety company authorized and licensed to do business in the state as surety, with the clerk of the circuit court in the county in which the dwelling unit is located in the total amount of the security deposits and advance rent he or she holds on behalf of the tenants or $50,000, whichever is less. The bond shall be conditioned upon the faithful compliance of the landlord with the provisions of this section and shall run to the Governor for the benefit of any tenant injured by the landlord's violation of the provisions of this section. In addition to posting the surety bond, the landlord shall pay to the tenant interest at the rate of 5 percent per year, simple interest. A landlord, or the landlord's agent, engaged in the renting of dwelling units in five or more counties, who holds deposit moneys or advance rent and who is otherwise subject to the provisions of this section, may, in lieu of posting a surety bond in each county, elect to post a surety bond in the form and manner provided in this paragraph with the office of the Secretary of State. The bond shall be in the total amount of the security deposit or advance rent held on behalf of tenants or in the amount of $250,000, whichever is less. The bond shall be conditioned upon the faithful compliance of the landlord with the provisions of this section and shall run to the Governor for the benefit of any tenant injured by the landlord's violation of this section. In addition to posting a surety bond, the landlord shall pay to the tenant interest on the security deposit or advance rent held on behalf of that tenant at the rate of 5 percent per year simple interest.

(2) The landlord shall, within 30 days of receipt of advance rent or a security deposit, notify the tenant in writing of the manner in which the landlord is holding the advance rent or security deposit and the rate of interest, if any, which the tenant is to receive and the time of interest payments to the tenant. Such written notice shall:

(a) Be given in person or by mail to the tenant.

(b) State the name and address of the depository where the advance rent or security deposit is being held, whether the advance rent or security deposit is being held in a separate account for the benefit of the tenant or is commingled with other funds of the landlord, and, if commingled, whether such funds are deposited in

(c) Include a copy of the provisions of subsection (3). Subsequent to providing such notice, if the landlord changes the manner or location in which he or she is holding the advance rent or security deposit, he or she shall notify the tenant within 30 days of the change according to the provisions herein set forth. This subsection does not apply to any landlord who rents fewer than five individual dwelling units. Failure to provide this notice shall not be a defense to the payment of rent when due.

(3)(a) Upon the vacating of the premises for termination of the lease, the landlord shall have 15 days to return the security deposit together with interest if otherwise required, or in which to give the tenant written notice by certified mail to the tenant's last known mailing address of his or her intention to impose a claim on the deposit and the reason for imposing the claim. The notice shall contain a statement in substantially the following form:

> This is a notice of my intention to impose a claim for damages in the amount of _____ upon your security deposit, due to _____. It is sent to you as required by s. 83.49(3), Florida Statutes. You are hereby notified that you must object in writing to this deduction from your security deposit within 15 days from the time you receive this notice or I will be authorized to deduct my claim from your security deposit. Your objection must be sent to (landlord's address).

If the landlord fails to give the required notice within the 15-day period, he or she forfeits the right to impose a claim upon the security deposit.

(b) Unless the tenant objects to the imposition of the landlord's claim or the amount thereof within 15 days after receipt of the landlord's notice of intention to impose a claim, the landlord may then deduct the amount of his or her claim and shall remit the balance of the deposit to the tenant within 30 days after the date of the notice of intention to impose a claim for damages.

(c) If either party institutes an action in a court of competent jurisdiction to adjudicate the party's right to the security deposit, the prevailing party is entitled to receive his or her court costs plus a reasonable fee for his or her attorney. The court shall advance the cause on the calendar.

(d) Compliance with this section by an individual or business entity authorized to conduct business in this state, including Florida-licensed real estate brokers and salespersons, shall constitute compliance with all other relevant Florida Statutes pertaining to security deposits held pursuant to a rental agreement or other landlord-tenant relationship. Enforcement personnel shall look solely to this section to determine compliance. This section prevails over any conflicting provisions in chapter 475 and in other sections of the Florida Statutes, and shall operate to permit licensed real estate brokers to disburse security deposits and deposit money without having to comply with the notice and settlement procedures contained in s. 475.25(1)(d).

(4) The provisions of this section do not apply to transient rentals by hotels or motels as defined in chapter 509; nor do they apply in those instances in which the amount of rent or deposit, or both, is regulated by law or by rules or regulations of a public body, including public housing authorities and federally administered or regulated housing programs including s. 202, s. 221(d)(3) and (4), s. 236, or s. 8 of the National Housing Act, as amended, other than for rent stabilization. With the exception of subsections (3), (5), and (6), this section is not applicable to housing authorities or public housing

(5) Except when otherwise provided by the terms of a written lease, any tenant who vacates or abandons the premises prior to the expiration of the term specified in the written lease, or any tenant who vacates or abandons premises which are the subject of a tenancy from week to week, month to month, quarter to quarter, or year to year, shall give at least 7 days' written notice by certified mail or personal delivery to the landlord prior to vacating or abandoning the premises which notice shall include the address where the tenant may be reached. Failure to give such notice shall relieve the landlord of the notice requirement of paragraph (3)(a) but shall not waive any right the tenant may have to the security deposit or any part of it.

(6) For the purposes of this part, a renewal of an existing rental agreement shall be considered a new rental agreement, and any security deposit carried forward shall be considered a new security deposit.

(7) Upon the sale or transfer of title of the rental property from one owner to another, or upon a change in the designated rental agent, any and all security deposits or advance rents being held for the benefit of the tenants shall be transferred to the new owner or agent, together with any earned interest and with an accurate accounting showing the amounts to be credited to each tenant account. Upon the transfer of such funds and records as stated herein, and upon transmittal of a written receipt therefor, the transferor shall be free from the obligation imposed in subsection (1) to hold such moneys on behalf of the tenant. However, nothing herein shall excuse the landlord or agent for a violation of the provisions of this section while in possession of such deposits.

(8) Any person licensed under the provisions of s. 509.241, unless excluded by the provisions of this part, who fails to comply with the provisions of this part shall be subject to a fine or to the suspension or revocation of his or her license by the Division of Hotels and Restaurants of the Department of Business and Professional Regulation in the manner provided in s. 509.261.

(9) In those cases in which interest is required to be paid to the tenant, the landlord shall pay directly to the tenant, or credit against the current month's rent, the interest due to the tenant at least once annually. However, no interest shall be due a tenant who wrongfully terminates his or her tenancy prior to the end of the rental term.

83.50 Disclosure.—

(1) The landlord, or a person authorized to enter into a rental agreement on the landlord's behalf, shall disclose in writing to the tenant, at or before the commencement of the tenancy, the name and address of the landlord or a person authorized to receive notices and demands in the landlord's behalf. The person so authorized to receive notices and demands retains authority until the tenant is notified otherwise. All notices of such names and addresses or changes thereto shall be delivered to the tenant's residence or, if specified in writing by the tenant, to any other address.

(2) The landlord or the landlord's authorized representative, upon completion of construction of a building exceeding three stories in height and containing dwelling units, shall disclose to the tenants initially moving into the building the availability or lack of availability of fire protection.

83.51 Landlord's obligation to maintain premises.—

(1) The landlord at all times during the tenancy shall:

(a) Comply with the requirements of applicable building, housing, and health codes; or

(b) Where there are no applicable building, housing, or health codes, maintain the roofs, windows, screens, doors, floors, steps, porches, exterior walls, foundations, and all other structural components in good repair and capable of resisting normal forces and loads and the plumbing in reasonable working condition. However, the landlord shall not be required to maintain a mobile home or other structure owned by the tenant. The landlord's obligations under this subsection may be altered or modified in writing with respect to a single-family home or duplex.

(2)(a) Unless otherwise agreed in writing, in addition to the requirements of subsection (1), the landlord of a dwelling unit other than a single-family home or duplex shall, at all times during the tenancy, make reasonable provisions for:

1. The extermination of rats, mice, roaches, ants, wood-destroying organisms, and bedbugs. When vacation of the premises is required for such extermination, the landlord shall not be liable for damages but shall abate the rent. The tenant shall be required to temporarily vacate the premises for a period of time not to exceed 4 days, on 7 days' written notice, if necessary, for extermination pursuant to this subparagraph.

2. Locks and keys.

3. The clean and safe condition of common areas.

4. Garbage removal and outside receptacles therefor.

5. Functioning facilities for heat during winter, running water, and hot water.

(b) Unless otherwise agreed in writing, at the commencement of the tenancy of a single-family home or duplex, the landlord shall install working smoke detection devices. As used in this paragraph, the term "smoke detection device" means an electrical or battery-operated device which detects visible or invisible particles of combustion and which is listed by Underwriters Laboratories, Inc., Factory Mutual Laboratories, Inc., or any other nationally recognized testing laboratory using nationally accepted testing standards.

(c) Nothing in this part authorizes the tenant to raise a noncompliance by the landlord with this subsection as a defense to an action for possession under s. 83.59.

(d) This subsection shall not apply to a mobile home owned by a tenant.

(e) Nothing contained in this subsection prohibits the landlord from providing in the rental agreement that the tenant is obligated to pay costs or charges for garbage removal, water, fuel, or utilities.

(3) If the duty imposed by subsection (1) is the same or greater than any duty imposed by subsection (2), the landlord's duty is determined by subsection (1).

(4) The landlord is not responsible to the tenant under this section for conditions created or caused by the negligent or wrongful act or omission of the tenant, a member of the tenant's family, or other person on the premises with the tenant's consent.

83.52 Tenant's obligation to maintain dwelling unit.—

The tenant at all times during the tenancy shall:

(1) Comply with all obligations imposed upon tenants by applicable provisions of building, housing, and health codes.

(2) Keep that part of the premises which he or she occupies and uses clean and sanitary.

(3) Remove from the tenant's dwelling unit all garbage in a clean and sanitary manner.

(4) Keep all plumbing fixtures in the dwelling unit or used by the tenant clean and sanitary and in repair.

(5) Use and operate in a reasonable manner all electrical, plumbing, sanitary, heating, ventilating, air-conditioning and other facilities and appliances, including elevators.

(6) Not destroy, deface, damage, impair, or remove any part of the premises or property therein belonging to the landlord nor permit any person to do so.

(7) Conduct himself or herself, and require other persons on the premises with his or her consent to conduct themselves, in a manner that does not unreasonably disturb the tenant's neighbors or constitute a breach of the peace.

83.53 Landlord's access to dwelling unit.—

(1) The tenant shall not unreasonably withhold consent to the landlord to enter the dwelling unit from time to time in order to inspect the premises; make necessary or agreed repairs, decorations, alterations, or improvements; supply agreed services; or exhibit the dwelling unit to prospective or actual purchasers, mortgagees, tenants, workers, or contractors.

(2) The landlord may enter the dwelling unit at any time for the protection or preservation of the premises. The landlord may enter the dwelling unit upon reasonable notice to the tenant and at a reasonable time for the purpose of repair of the premises. "Reasonable notice" for the purpose of repair is notice given at least 12 hours prior to the entry, and reasonable time for the purpose of repair shall be between the hours of 7:30 a.m. and 8:00 p.m. The landlord may enter the dwelling unit when necessary for the further purposes set forth in subsection (1) under any of the following circumstances:

(a) With the consent of the tenant;

(b) In case of emergency;

(c) When the tenant unreasonably withholds consent; or

(d) If the tenant is absent from the premises for a period of time equal to one-half the time for periodic rental payments. If the rent is current and the tenant notifies the landlord of an intended absence, then the landlord may enter only with the consent of the tenant or for the protection or preservation of the premises.

(3) The landlord shall not abuse the right of access nor use it to harass the tenant.

83.535 Flotation bedding system; restrictions on use.—

No landlord may prohibit a tenant from using a flotation bedding system in a dwelling unit, provided the flotation bedding system does not violate applicable building codes. The tenant shall be required to carry in the tenant's name flotation insurance as is standard in the industry in an amount deemed reasonable to protect the tenant and owner against personal injury and property damage to the dwelling units. In any case, the policy shall carry a loss payable clause to the owner of the building.

83.54 Enforcement of rights and duties; civil action.—

Any right or duty declared in this part is enforceable by civil action.

83.55 Right of action for damages.—

If either the landlord or the tenant fails to comply with the requirements of the rental agreement or this part, the aggrieved party may recover the damages caused by the noncompliance.

83.56 Termination of rental agreement.—

(1) If the landlord materially fails to comply with s. 83.51(1) or material provisions of the rental agreement within 7 days after delivery of written notice by the tenant specifying the noncompliance and indicating the intention of the tenant to terminate the rental agreement by reason thereof, the tenant may terminate the rental agreement. If the failure to comply with s. 83.51(1) or material provisions of the rental agreement is due to causes beyond the control of the landlord and the landlord has made and continues to make every reasonable effort to correct the failure to comply, the rental agreement may be terminated or altered by the parties, as follows:

(a) If the landlord's failure to comply renders the dwelling unit untenantable and the tenant vacates, the tenant shall not be liable for rent during the period the dwelling unit remains uninhabitable.

(b) If the landlord's failure to comply does not render the dwelling unit untenantable and the tenant remains in occupancy, the rent for the period of noncompliance shall be reduced by an amount in proportion to the loss of rental value caused by the noncompliance.

(2) If the tenant materially fails to comply with s. 83.52 or material provisions of the rental agreement, other than a failure to pay rent, or reasonable rules or regulations, the landlord may:

(a) If such noncompliance is of a nature that the tenant should not be given an opportunity to cure it or if the noncompliance constitutes a subsequent or continuing noncompliance within 12 months of a written warning by the landlord of a similar violation, deliver a written notice to the tenant specifying the noncompliance and the landlord's intent to terminate the rental agreement by reason thereof. Examples of noncompliance which are of a nature that the tenant should not be given an opportunity to cure include, but are not limited to, destruction, damage, or misuse of the landlord's or other tenants' property by intentional act or a subsequent or continued unreasonable disturbance. In such event, the landlord may terminate the rental agreement, and the tenant shall have 7 days from the date that the notice is delivered to vacate the premises. The notice shall be adequate if it is in substantially the following form:

You are advised that your lease is terminated effective immediately. You shall have 7 days from the delivery of this letter to vacate the premises. This action is taken because (cite the noncompliance).

(b) If such noncompliance is of a nature that the tenant should be given an opportunity to cure it, deliver a written notice to the tenant specifying the noncompliance, including a notice that, if the noncompliance is not corrected within 7 days from the date the written notice is delivered, the landlord shall terminate the rental agreement by reason thereof. Examples of such noncompliance include, but are not limited to, activities in contravention of the lease or this act such as having or permitting unauthorized pets, guests, or vehicles; parking in an unauthorized manner or permitting such parking; or failing to keep the premises clean and sanitary. The notice shall be adequate if it is in substantially the following form:

You are hereby notified that (cite the noncompliance), Demand is hereby made that you remedy the noncompliance within 7 days of receipt of this notice or your lease shall be deemed terminated and you shall vacate the premises upon such termination. If this same conduct or conduct of a similar nature is repeated within 12 months, your tenancy is subject to termination without your being given an opportunity to cure the noncompliance.

(3) If the tenant fails to pay rent when due and the default continues for 3 days, excluding Saturday, Sunday, and legal holidays, after delivery of written demand by the landlord for payment of the rent or possession of the premises, the landlord may terminate the rental agreement. Legal holidays for the purpose of this section shall be court-observed holidays only. The 3-day notice shall contain a statement in substantially the following form:

> You are hereby notified that you are indebted to me in the sum of _____ dollars for the rent and use of the premises (address of leased premises, including county), Florida, now occupied by you and that I demand payment of the rent or possession of the premises within 3 days (excluding Saturday, Sunday, and legal holidays) from the date of delivery of this notice, to wit: on or before the _____ day of _____, 19_____. (landlord's name, address and phone number)

(4) The delivery of the written notices required by subsections (1), (2), and (3) shall be by mailing or delivery of a true copy thereof or, if the tenant is absent from the premises, by leaving a copy thereof at the residence.

(5) If the landlord accepts rent with actual knowledge of a noncompliance by the tenant or accepts performance by the tenant of any other provision of the rental agreement that is at variance with its provisions, or if the tenant pays rent with actual knowledge of a noncompliance by the landlord or accepts performance by the landlord of any other provision of the rental agreement that is at variance with its provisions, the landlord or tenant waives his or her right to terminate the rental agreement or to bring a civil action for that noncompliance, but not for any subsequent or continuing noncompliance. Any tenant who wishes to defend against an action by the landlord for possession of the unit for noncompliance of the rental agreement or of relevant statutes shall comply with the provisions in s. 83.60(2). The court may not set a date for mediation or trial unless the provisions of s. 83.60(2) have been met, but shall enter a default judgment for removal of the tenant with a writ of possession to issue immediately if the tenant fails to comply with s. 83.60(2). This subsection does not apply to that portion of rent subsidies received from a local, state, or national government or an agency of local, state, or national government; however, waiver will occur if an action has not been instituted within 45 days of the noncompliance.

(6) If the rental agreement is terminated, the landlord shall comply with s. 83.49(3).

83.57 Termination of tenancy without specific term.—

A tenancy without a specific duration, as defined in s. 83.46(2) or (3), may be terminated by either party giving written notice in the manner provided in s. 83.56(4), as follows:

(1) When the tenancy is from year to year, by giving not less than 60 days' notice prior to the end of any annual period;

(2) When the tenancy is from quarter to quarter, by giving not less than 30 days' notice prior to the end of any quarterly period;

(3) When the tenancy is from month to month, by giving not less than 15 days' notice prior to the end of any monthly period; and

(4) When the tenancy is from week to week, by giving not less than 7 days' notice prior to the end of any weekly period.

83.58 Remedies; tenant holding over.—

If the tenant holds over and continues in possession of the dwelling unit or any part thereof after the expiration of the rental agreement without the permission of the landlord, the landlord may recover possession of the dwelling unit in the manner provided for in s. 83.59 [F.S. 1973]. The landlord may also recover double the amount of rent due on the dwelling unit, or any part thereof, for the period during which the tenant refuses to surrender possession.

83.59 Right of action for possession.—

(1) If the rental agreement is terminated and the tenant does not vacate the premises, the landlord may recover possession of the dwelling unit as provided in this section.

(2) A landlord, the landlord's attorney, or the landlord's agent, applying for the removal of a tenant shall file in the county court of the county where the premises are situated a complaint describing the dwelling unit and stating the facts that authorize its recovery. A landlord's agent is not permitted to take any action other than the initial filing of the complaint, unless the landlord's agent is an attorney. The landlord is entitled to the summary procedure provided in s. 51.011 [F.S. 1971], and the court shall advance the cause on the calendar.

(3) The landlord shall not recover possession of a dwelling unit except:

(a) In an action for possession under subsection (2) or other civil action in which the issue of right of possession is determined;

(b) When the tenant has surrendered possession of the dwelling unit to the landlord; or

(c) When the tenant has abandoned the dwelling unit. In the absence of actual knowledge of abandonment, it shall be presumed that the tenant has abandoned the dwelling unit if he or she is absent from the premises for a period of time equal to one-half the time for periodic rental payments. However, this presumption shall not apply if the rent is current or the tenant has notified the landlord, in writing, of an intended absence.

(4) The prevailing party is entitled to have judgment for costs and execution therefor.

83.60 Defenses to action for rent or possession; procedure.—

(1) In an action by the landlord for possession of a dwelling unit based upon nonpayment of rent or in an action by the landlord under s. 83.55 seeking to recover unpaid rent, the tenant may defend upon the ground of a material noncompliance with s. 83.51(1) [F.S. 1973], or may raise any other defense, whether legal or equitable, that he or she may have, including the defense of retaliatory conduct in accordance with s. 83.64. The defense of a material noncompliance with s. 83.51(1) [F.S. 1973] may be raised by the tenant if 7 days have elapsed after the delivery of written notice by the tenant to the landlord, specifying the noncompliance and indicating the intention of the tenant not to pay rent by reason thereof. Such notice by the tenant may be given to the landlord, the landlord's representative as designated pursuant to s. 83.50(1), a resident manager, or the person or entity who collects the rent on behalf of the landlord. A material noncompliance with s. 83.51(1) [F.S. 1973] by the landlord is a complete defense to an action for possession based upon nonpayment of rent, and, upon hearing, the court or the jury, as the case may be, shall determine the amount, if any, by which the rent is to be reduced to reflect the diminution in value of the dwelling unit during the period of noncompliance with s. 83.51(1) [F.S. 1973]. After consideration of all other relevant issues, the court shall enter appropriate judgment.

(2) In an action by the landlord for possession of a dwelling unit, if the tenant interposes any defense other than payment, the tenant shall pay into the registry of the court the accrued rent as alleged in the complaint or as determined by the court and the rent which accrues during the pendency of the proceeding, when due. The clerk shall notify the tenant of

such requirement in the summons. Failure of the tenant to pay the rent into the registry of the court or to file a motion to determine the amount of rent to be paid into the registry within 5 days, excluding Saturdays, Sundays, and legal holidays, after the date of service of process constitutes an absolute waiver of the tenant's defenses other than payment, and the landlord is entitled to an immediate default judgment for removal of the tenant with a writ of possession to issue without further notice or hearing thereon. In the event a motion to determine rent is filed, documentation in support of the allegation that the rent as alleged in the complaint is in error is required. Public housing tenants or tenants receiving rent subsidies shall be required to deposit only that portion of the full rent for which the tenant is responsible pursuant to federal, state, or local program in which they are participating.

83.61 Disbursement of funds in registry of court; prompt final hearing.—

When the tenant has deposited funds into the registry of the court in accordance with the provisions of s. 83.60(2) and the landlord is in actual danger of loss of the premises or other personal hardship resulting from the loss of rental income from the premises, the landlord may apply to the court for disbursement of all or part of the funds or for prompt final hearing. The court shall advance the cause on the calendar. The court, after preliminary hearing, may award all or any portion of the funds on deposit to the landlord or may proceed immediately to a final resolution of the cause.

83.62 Restoration of possession to landlord.—

(1) In an action for possession, after entry of judgment in favor of the landlord, the clerk shall issue a writ to the sheriff describing the premises and commanding the sheriff to put the landlord in possession after 24 hours' notice conspicuously posted on the premises.

(2) At the time the sheriff executes the writ of possession or at any time thereafter, the landlord or the landlord's agent may remove any personal property found on the premises to or near the property line. Subsequent to executing the writ of possession, the landlord may request the sheriff to stand by to keep the peace while the landlord changes the locks and removes the personal property from the premises. When such a request is made, the sheriff may charge a reasonable hourly rate, and the person requesting the sheriff to stand by to keep the peace shall be responsible for paying the reasonable hourly rate set by the sheriff. Neither the sheriff nor the landlord or the landlord's agent shall be liable to the tenant or any other party for the loss, destruction, or damage to the property after it has been removed.

83.625 Power to award possession and enter money judgment.—

In an action by the landlord for possession of a dwelling unit based upon nonpayment of rent, if the court finds the rent is due, owing, and unpaid and by reason thereof the landlord is entitled to possession of the premises, the court, in addition to awarding possession of the premises to the landlord, shall direct, in an amount which is within its jurisdictional limitations, the entry of a money judgment with costs in favor of the landlord and against the tenant for the amount of money found due, owing, and unpaid by the tenant to the landlord. However, no money judgment shall be entered unless service of process has been effected by personal service or, where authorized by law, by certified or registered mail, return receipt, or in any other manner prescribed by law or the rules of the court; and no money judgment may be entered except in compliance with the Florida Rules of Civil Procedure. The prevailing party in the action may also be awarded attorney's fees and costs.

83.63 Casualty damage.—

If the premises are damaged or destroyed other than by the wrongful or negligent acts of the tenant so that the enjoyment of the premises is substantially impaired, the tenant may terminate the rental agreement and immediately vacate the premises. The tenant may vacate the part of the premises rendered unusable by the casualty, in which case the tenant's liability for rent shall be reduced by the fair rental value of that part of the premises damaged or destroyed. If the rental agreement is terminated, the landlord shall comply with s. 83.49(3) [F.S. 1973].

83.64 Retaliatory conduct.—

(1) It is unlawful for a landlord to discriminatorily increase a tenant's rent or decrease services to a tenant, or to bring or threaten to bring an action for possession or other civil action, primarily because the landlord is retaliating against the tenant. In order for the tenant to raise the defense of retaliatory conduct, the tenant must have acted in good faith. Examples of conduct for which the landlord may not retaliate include, but are not limited to, situations where:

(a) The tenant has complained to a governmental agency charged with responsibility for enforcement of a building, housing, or health code of a suspected violation applicable to the premises;

(b) The tenant has organized, encouraged, or participated in a tenants' organization; or

(c) The tenant has complained to the landlord pursuant to s. 83.56(1).

(2) Evidence of retaliatory conduct may be raised by the tenant as a defense in any action brought against him or her for possession.

(3) In any event, this section does not apply if the landlord proves that the eviction is for good cause. Examples of good cause include, but are not limited to, good faith actions for nonpayment of rent, violation of the rental agreement or of reasonable rules, or violation of the terms of this chapter.

(4) "Discrimination" under this section means that a tenant is being treated differently as to the rent charged, the services rendered, or the action being taken by the landlord, which shall be a prerequisite to a finding of retaliatory conduct.

83.67 Prohibited practices.—

(1) No landlord of any dwelling unit governed by this part shall cause, directly or indirectly, the termination or interruption of any utility service furnished the tenant, including, but not limited to, water, heat, light, electricity, gas, elevator, garbage collection, or refrigeration, whether or not the utility service is under the control

(2) No landlord of any dwelling unit governed by this part shall prevent the tenant from gaining reasonable access to the dwelling unit by any means, including, but not limited to, changing the locks or using any bootlock or similar device.

(3) No landlord of any dwelling unit governed by this part shall remove the outside doors, locks, roof, walls, or windows of the unit except for purposes of maintenance, repair, or replacement; nor shall the landlord remove the tenant's personal property from the dwelling unit unless said action is taken after surrender, abandonment, or a lawful eviction. If provided in the rental agreement or a written agreement separate from the rental agreement, upon surrender or abandonment by the tenant, the landlord shall not be liable or responsible for storage or disposition of the tenant's personal property; if provided in the rental agreement there shall be printed or clearly stamped on such rental agreement a legend in substantially the following form:

> BY SIGNING THIS RENTAL AGREEMENT THE TENANT AGREES THAT UPON SURRENDER OR ABANDONMENT, AS DEFINED BY THE FLORIDA STATUTES, THE LANDLORD SHALL NOT BE LIABLE OR RESPONSIBLE FOR STORAGE OR DISPOSITION OF THE TENANT'S PERSONAL PROPERTY.

For the purposes of this section, abandonment shall be as set forth in s. 83.59(3)(c).

(4) A landlord who violates the provisions of this section shall be liable to the tenant for actual and consequential damages or 3 months' rent, whichever is greater, and costs, including attorney's fees. Subsequent or repeated violations which are not contemporaneous with the initial violation shall be subject to separate awards of damages.

(5) A violation of this section shall constitute irreparable harm for the purposes of injunctive relief.

(6) The remedies provided by this section are not exclusive and shall not preclude the tenant from pursuing any other remedy at law or equity which the tenant may have.

83.681 Orders to enjoin violations of this part.—

(1) A landlord who gives notice to a tenant of the landlord's intent to terminate the tenant's lease pursuant to s. 83.56(2)(a), due to the tenant's intentional destruction, damage, or misuse of the landlord's property may petition the county or circuit court for an injunction prohibiting the tenant from continuing to violate any of the provisions of that part.

(2) The court shall grant the relief requested pursuant to subsection (1) in conformity with the principles that govern the granting of injunctive relief from threatened loss or damage in other civil cases.

(3) Evidence of a tenant's intentional destruction, damage, or misuse of the landlord's property in an amount greater than twice the value of money deposited with the landlord pursuant to s. 83.49 or $300, whichever is greater, shall constitute irreparable harm for the purposes of injunctive relief.

APPENDIX 2:

LEASE ARBITRATION CLAUSE

It is hereby agreed by and between the parties to the Lease, that if at any time during the term of the Lease there shall arise a dispute relating to any provision of said Lease, or to the rights and responsibilities of the parties to said Lease, such dispute shall be submitted to the American Arbitration Association for a determination of the dispute, and the parties agree that said determination shall be binding upon the parties.

APPENDIX 3:

RESIDENTIAL LEASE—SHORT FORM

THIS AGREEMENT, is made this _____ day of _____, 19__ between [Name of Landlord] ("Landlord") and [Name of Tenant] ("Tenant").

For good and valuable consideration, it is agreed between the above-named parties as follows:

1. Landlord hereby leases and lets to Tenant the premises described as follows: [Insert address of property being leased].

2. This Lease shall be for a term of [Insert term, e.g., # years, # months, etc.], commencing on [Commencement Date] and terminating on [Termination Date].

3. Tenant shall pay Landlord the rent of [Specify dollar amount and manner in which payments are to be made, e.g. Seven Hundred Dollars per month, payable on the first day of each month in advance].

4. Tenant shall pay a security deposit of [Dollar Amount ($xxx)] dollars, which amount shall be held in an interest-bearing account in [Name and Address of Bank], to be returned upon termination of this lease and full performance of all obligations hereunder, including the payment of all rent due.

5. Tenant shall at his/her own expense provide the following utilities: [Specify which utilities Tenant shall be liable for, e.g. electricity, gas, water, etc.].

6. Landlord shall at its own expense provide the following utilities: [Specify which utilities Landlord shall be liable for, e.g. electricity, gas, water, etc.].

7. Tenant further agrees that upon the termination of the Lease Tenant will return possession of the leased premises in its present condition, reasonable wear and tear excepted. Further, Tenant shall commit no waste to the leased premises.

8. Tenant shall not assign or sublet said premises or allow any other person to occupy the leased premises without Landlord's prior written consent, which consent shall not be unreasonably withheld.

9. Tenant shall not make any material or structural alterations to the leased premises without Landlord's prior written consent.

10. Tenant shall comply with all building, zoning and health codes and other applicable laws for the use of said leased premises.

11. Tenant shall not conduct on premises hazardous activities, or activities deemed a nuisance.

12. Tenant shall not allow pets on the premises [alternative language: except those specifically set forth herein].

13. In the event of any breach of the payment of rent or other breach of this Lease, Landlord shall have full rights to terminate this Lease in accordance with the applicable state law, and enter and reclaim possession of the leased premises, in addition to any other remedies available to Landlord arising from said breach.

14. This Lease shall be binding upon and inure to the benefit of the parties, their successors, assigns and personal representatives.

15. This Lease shall be subordinate to all present or future mortgages against the property.

16. [Set forth any additional terms agreed to between the parties].

BY:

[SIGNATURE LINE—LANDLORD]

BY:

[SIGNATURE LINE—TENANT]

In the presence of:

[SIGNATURE LINE—WITNESS]

APPENDIX 4:

SUBLEASE

THIS AGREEMENT, is made this _____day of _____, 19__ between [Name of Landlord] ("Landlord") and [Name of Tenant] ("Tenant"), and [Name of Subtenant] ("Subtenant").

For good and valuable consideration, it is agreed between the above-named parties as follows:

1. The Tenant agrees to sublease to the Subtenant the premises described as follows: [Insert address of property being leased].

2. The Subtenant agrees to comply with all terms and conditions of the original lease entered into between Tenant and Landlord on [Insert Date of Original Lease], including the prompt payment of all rents. Those lease terms are incorporated into this agreement by reference.

3. The Subtenant agrees to pay the Landlord the monthly rent stated in that lease, and all other rental charges hereinafter due, and otherwise assume all of Tenant's obligations during the Sublease period and indemnify Tenant from same.

4. The Subtenant agrees to pay to Tenant the sum of [Dollar Amount ($xxx)] Dollars as a security deposit, to be promptly returned upon the termination of this sublease and compliance of all its conditions.

5. Attached to this agreement is an inventory of items or fixtures located on the above described property as of [Insert Date]. The Subtenant agrees to replace or reimburse the Tenant for any of these items that are missing or damaged at the time Tenant takes repossession of the premises.

6. The Landlord consents to this sublease and agrees to promptly notify the Tenant if the Subtenant is in breach of this agreement.

7. Nothing herein shall constitute a release of Tenant who shall remain bound under the original lease.

8. Nothing herein shall constitute a consent to any further Sublease or Assignment of Lease.

9. [Set forth any additional terms agreed to between the parties].

BY:

[SIGNATURE LINE—LANDLORD]

BY:

[SIGNATURE LINE—TENANT]

BY:

[SIGNATURE LINE—SUBTENANT]

In the presence of:

[SIGNATURE LINE—WITNESS]

APPENDIX 5:

WARRANTY OF HABITABILITY—NEW YORK STATE

ARTICLE 7—Landlord and Tenant

SECTION 235-b. Warranty of habitability.

1. In every written or oral lease or rental agreement for residential premises the landlord or lessor shall be deemed to covenant and warrant that the premises so leased or rented and all areas used in connection therewith in common with other tenants or residents are fit for human habitation and for the uses reasonably intended by the parties and that the occupants of such premises shall not be subjected to any conditions which would be dangerous, hazardous or detrimental to their life, health or safety. When any such condition has been caused by the misconduct of the tenant or lessee or persons under his direction or control, it shall not constitute a breach of such covenants and warranties.

2. Any agreement by a lessee or tenant of a dwelling waiving or modifying his rights as set forth in this section shall be void as contrary to public policy.

3. In determining the amount of damages sustained by a tenant as a result of a breach of the warranty set forth in the section, the court;

   (a) need not require any expert testimony; and

   (b) shall, to the extent the warranty is breached or cannot be cured by reason of a strike or other labor dispute which is not caused primarily by the individual landlord or lessor and such damages are attributable to such strike, exclude recovery to such extent, except to the extent of the net savings, if any, to the landlord or lessor by reason of such strike or labor dispute allocable to the tenant's premises, provided, however, that the landlord or lesser has made a good faith attempt, where practicable, to cure the breach.

APPENDIX 6:

COMPLAINT BY TENANT
FOR BREACH OF WARRANTY OF HABITABILITY

NAME OF COURT

NAME OF JURISDICTION

COMPLAINT

Plaintiff, John Jones, by his attorney, _____, as and for his Complaint against the defendant, alleges as follows:

1. At all times hereinafter mentioned, plaintiff was a resident of the County of _____, State of _____.

2. At all times hereinafter mentioned, defendant was a resident of the County of _____, State of _____.

3. At all times hereinafter mentioned, defendant was the owner of a residential apartment building located at

_____.

4. At all times hereinafter mentioned, plaintiff was a tenant of the defendant, and occupied an apartment known as _____, located on the fifth floor of said apartment building.

5. At all times hereinafter mentioned, the defendant breached its warranty of habitability of the leased premises in that the ceiling tiles located in the living room of said apartment were loose, and that this condition had been in existence prior to the occurrence herein complained of, and that defendant had actual and constructive knowledge of this problem.

6. On _____, 19____, plaintiff was sitting in his living room when one of the ceiling tiles fell on his head, causing him to suffer severe injuries to his head and neck, all or some of which may be permanent.

7. Said injuries were caused by the failure of defendant to properly maintain the premises, and defendant's breach of warranty of habitability of the leased premises.

8. The plaintiff in no way contributed to his injuries.

WHEREFORE, plaintiff seeks judgment against the defendant in the sum of _____ ($_____) Dollars, together with the costs and disbursements of this action, and for such other and further relief as the Court deems proper.

BY:

[SIGNATURE LINE—ATTORNEY FOR PLAINTIFF]

APPENDIX 7:

COVENANT OF QUIET ENJOYMENT OF LEASED PREMISES

Landlord hereby covenants, warrants and represents to Tenant that, upon payment of the rent and observing all provisions herein required by this Lease, Tenant shall have the right to quietly and peaceably have, hold and enjoy the premises during the term set forth in the Lease.

APPENDIX 8:

NOTICE TO LANDLORD OF TENANT'S INTENTION TO VACATE LEASED PREMISES

[Date]

[Via Certified Mail—Return Receipt Requested]

Landlord's Name

Street Address

City, State Zip Code

Re: Notice of Intention to Vacate Leased Premises Located at [Address]

As set forth in our lease dated _____, I hereby notify you of my intention to vacate said premises on _____, 1998.

Please forward the security deposit to me in care of the following address: _____.

By:_____

[Signature Line—Tenant]

APPENDIX 9:

THREE-DAY NOTICE TO TENANT TO VACATE THE LEASED PREMISES DUE TO NON-PAYMENT OF RENT

[Date]

[Via Certified Mail—Return Receipt Requested]

Tenant's Name

Street Address

City, State Zip Code

Re: Three-Day Notice to Vacate Leased Premises Located at [Address]

You are hereby notified to surrender the above-referenced leased premises you occupy as our tenant and to vacate said premises on or within three days of your receipt of this notice, as a consequence of your non-payment of rent due under the lease.

The present rent due and owing in connection with said lease is _____ [$_____] Dollars. This notice may be rescinded upon full payment of said amount within three days of your receipt of this notice.

If you fail to pay all rent payments due and owing, we will have no recourse but to seek immediate legal action to evict you from said premises and to seek damages and attorneys' fees and costs as prescribed by law.

By:_____

[Signature Line—Landlord]

APPENDIX 10:

DIRECTORY OF HUD FAIR HOUSING OFFICES

AREAS COVERED	NAME	ADDRESS	LOCAL TELEPHONE	TOLL-FREE TELEPHONE	TTY
Connecticut, Maine, Massachusetts, New Hampshire, Rhode Island and Vermont	U.S. Department of Housing and Urban Development	Thomas P. O'Neill, Jr. Federal Building, 10 Causeway Street, Room 321, Boston, MA 02222-1092	(617) 565-5308	1-800-827-5005	(617) 565-5453
New Jersey and New York	U.S. Department of Housing and Urban Development	26 Federal Plaza, Room 3532, New York, NY 10278-0068	(212) 264-9610	1-800-496-4294	(212) 264-0927
Delaware, District of Columbia, Maryland, Pennsylvania, Virginia and West Virginia	U.S. Department of Housing and Urban Development	The Wanamaker Building, 100 Penn Square East, Philadelphia,PA 19107-3380	(215) 656-0660	1-888-799-2085	(215) 656-3450
Alabama, the Caribbean, Florida, Georgia, Kentucky, Mississippi, North Carolina, South Carolina and Tennessee	U.S. Department of Housing and Urban Development	Richard B. Russell Federal Building, 75 Spring Street SW, Room 230, Atlanta, Georgia 30303-3388	(404) 331-5140	1-800-440-8091	(404) 730-2654
Illinois, Indiana, Michigan, Minnesota, Ohio and Wisconsin	U.S. Department of Housing and Urban Development	Ralph H. Metcalfe Federal Building, 77 West Jackson Boulevard, Room 2101, Chicago, Illinois 60604-3507	(312) 353-7776	1-800-765-9372	(312) 353-7143

AREAS COVERED	NAME	ADDRESS	LOCAL TELEPHONE	TOLL-FREE TELEPHONE	TTY
Arkansas, Louisiana, New Mexico, Oklahoma and Texas	U.S. Department of Housing and Urban Development	1600 Throckmorton, Room 502, Fort Worth, Texas 76113-2905	(817) 978-9270	1-800-498-9371	(817) 978-9274
Iowa, Kansas, Missouri and Nebraska	U.S. Department of Housing and Urban Development	Gateway Tower II, 400 State Avenue, Room 200, Kansas City, Kansas 66101-2406	(913) 551-6958	1-800-743-5323	(913) 551-6972
Colorado, Montana, North Dakota, South Dakota, Utah and Wyoming	U.S. Department of Housing and Urban Development	633 17th Street, Denver, Colorado 80202-3607	(303) 672-5437	1-800-877-7353	(303) 672-5248
Arizona, California, Hawaii and Nevada	U.S. Department of Housing and Urban Development	Phillip Burton Federal Building and U.S. Courthouse, 450 Golden Gate Avenue, San Francisco, California 94102-3448	(415) 436-8400	1-800-347-3739	(415) 436-6594
Alaska, Idaho, Oregon and Washington	U.S. Department of Housing and Urban Development	Seattle Federal Office Building, 909 First Avenue, Room 205, Seattle, Washington 98104-1000	(206) 220-5170	1-800-877-0246	(206) 220-5185

SELECTED PROVISIONS OF THE FAIR HOUSING ACT

THE UNITED STATES CODE

TITLE 42—THE PUBLIC HEALTH AND WELFARE

CHAPTER 45—FAIR HOUSING

SUBCHAPTER I—GENERALLY

SECTION 3601. Declaration of policy

It is the policy of the United States to provide, within constitutional limitations, for fair housing throughout the United States.

SECTION 3602. Definitions

As used in this subchapter—

(a) "Secretary" means the Secretary of Housing and Urban Development.

(b) "Dwelling" means any building, structure, or portion thereof which is occupied as, or designed or intended for occupancy as, a residence by one or more families, and any vacant land which is offered for sale or lease for the construction or location thereon of any such building, structure, or portion thereof.

(c) "Family" includes a single individual.

(d) "Person" includes one or more individuals, corporations, partnerships, associations, labor organizations, legal representatives, mutual companies, joint-stock companies, trusts, unincorporated organizations, trustees, trustees in cases under title 11, receivers, and fiduciaries.

(e) "To rent" includes to lease, to sublease, to let and otherwise to grant for a consideration the right to occupy premises not owned by the occupant.

(f) "Discriminatory housing practice" means an act that is unlawful under section 3604, 3605, 3606, or 3617 of this title.

(g) "State" means any of the several States, the District of Columbia, the Commonwealth of Puerto Rico, or any of the territories and possessions of the United States.

(h) "Handicap" means, with respect to a person—(1) a physical or mental impairment which substantially limits one or more of such person's major life activities, (2) a record of having such an impairment, or (3) being regarded as having such an impairment, but such term does not include current, illegal use of or addiction to a controlled substance (as defined in section 802 of title 21).

(i) "Aggrieved person" includes any person who—(1) claims to have been injured by a discriminatory housing practice; or (2) believes that such person will be injured by a discriminatory housing practice that is about to occur.

(j) "Complainant" means the person (including the Secretary) who files a complaint under section 3610 of this title.

(k) "Familial status" means one or more individuals (who have not attained the age of 18 years) being domiciled with—(1) a parent or another person having legal custody of such individual or individuals; or (2) the designee of such parent or other person having such custody, with the written permission of such parent or other person. The protections afforded against discrimination on the basis of familial status shall apply to any person who is pregnant or is in the process of securing legal custody of any individual who has not attained the age of 18 years.

(l) "Conciliation" means the attempted resolution of issues raised by a complaint, or by the investigation of such complaint, through informal negotiations involving the aggrieved person, the respondent, and the Secretary.

(m) "Conciliation agreement" means a written agreement setting forth the resolution of the issues in conciliation.

(n) "Respondent" means—(1) the person or other entity accused in a complaint of an unfair housing practice; and (2) any other person or entity identified in the course of investigation and notified as required with respect to respondents so identified under section 3610(a) of this title.

(o) "Prevailing party" has the same meaning as such term has in section 1988 of this title.

SECTION 3604. Discrimination in the sale or rental of housing and other prohibited practices

As made applicable by section 3603 of this title and except as exempted by sections 3603(b) and 3607 of this title, it shall be unlawful—

(a) To refuse to sell or rent after the making of a bona fide offer, or to refuse to negotiate for the sale or rental of, or otherwise make unavailable or deny, a dwelling to any person because of race, color, religion, sex, familial status, or national origin.

(b) To discriminate against any person in the terms, conditions, or privileges of sale or rental of a dwelling, or in the provision of services or facilities in connection therewith, because of, race, color, religion, sex, familial status, or national origin.

(c) To make, print, or publish, or cause to be made, printed, or published any notice, statement, or advertisement, with respect to the sale or rental of a dwelling that indicates any preference, limitation, or discrimination based on race, color, religion, sex, handicap, familial status, or national origin, or an intention to make any such preference, limitation, or discrimination.

(d) To represent to any person because of race, color, religion, sex, handicap, familial status, or national origin that any dwelling is not available for inspection, sale, or rental when such dwelling is in fact so available.

(e) For profit, to induce or attempt to induce any person to sell or rent any dwelling by representations regarding the entry or prospective entry into the neighborhood of a person or persons of a particular race, color, religion, sex, handicap, familial status, or national origin.

(f)(1) To discriminate in the sale or rental, or to otherwise make unavailable or deny, a dwelling to any buyer or renter because of a handicap of—

(A) that buyer or renter;

(B) a person residing in or intending to reside in that dwelling after it is so sold, rented, or made available; or

(C) any person associated with that buyer or renter.

(f)(2) To discriminate against any person in the terms, conditions, or privileges of sale or rental of a dwelling, or in the provision of services or facilities in connection with such dwelling, because of a handicap of—

(A) that person; or

(B) a person residing in or intending to reside in that dwelling after it is so sold, rented, or made available; or

(C) any person associated with that person.

(f)(3) For purposes of this subsection, discrimination includes

(A) a refusal to permit, at the expense of the handicapped person, reasonable modifications of existing premises occupied or to be occupied by such person if such modifications may be necessary to afford such person full enjoyment of the premises except that, in the case of a rental, the landlord may where it is reasonable to do so condition permission for a modification on the renter agreeing to restore the interior of the premises to the condition that existed before the modification, reasonable wear and tear excepted;

(B) a refusal to make reasonable accommodations in rules, policies, practices, or services, when such accommodations may be necessary to afford such person equal opportunity to use and enjoy a dwelling; or

(C) in connection with the design and construction of covered multifamily dwellings for first occupancy after the date that is 30 months after September 13, 1988, a failure to design and construct those dwellings in such a manner that—

(i) the public use and common use portions of such dwellings are readily accessible to and usable by handicapped persons;

(ii) all the doors designed to allow passage into and within all premises within such dwellings are sufficiently wide to allow passage by handicapped persons in wheelchairs; and

(iii) all premises within such dwellings contain the following features of adaptive design:

(I) an accessible route into and through the dwelling;

(II) light switches, electrical outlets, thermostats, and other environmental controls in accessible locations;

(III) reinforcements in bathroom walls to allow later installation of grab bars; and

(IV) usable kitchens and bathrooms such that an individual in a wheelchair can maneuver about the space.

(f)(4) Compliance with the appropriate requirements of the American National Standard for buildings and facilities providing accessibility and usability for physically handicapped people (commonly cited as "ANSI A117.1") suffices to satisfy the requirements of paragraph (3)(C)(iii).

(f)(5)(A) If a State or unit of general local government has incorporated into its laws the requirements set forth in paragraph (3)(C), compliance with such laws shall be deemed to satisfy the requirements of that paragraph.

(f)(5)(B) A State or unit of general local government may review and approve newly constructed covered multifamily dwellings for the purpose of making determinations as to whether the design and construction requirements of paragraph (3)(C) are met.

(f)(5)(C) The Secretary shall encourage, but may not require, States and units of local government to include in their existing procedures for the review and approval of newly constructed covered multifamily dwellings, determinations as to whether the design and construction of such dwellings are consistent with paragraph (3)(C), and shall provide technical assistance to States and units of local government and other persons to implement the requirements of paragraph (3)(C).

(f)(5)(D) Nothing in this subchapter shall be construed to require the Secretary to review or approve the plans, designs or construction of all covered multifamily dwellings, to determine whether the design and construction of such dwellings are consistent with the requirements of paragraph 3(C).

(f)(6)(A) Nothing in paragraph (5) shall be construed to affect the authority and responsibility of the Secretary or a State or local public agency certified pursuant to section 3610(f)(3) of this title to receive and process complaints or otherwise engage in enforcement activities under this subchapter.

(f)(6)(B) Determinations by a State or a unit of general local government under paragraphs (5)(A) and (B) shall not be conclusive in enforcement proceedings under this subchapter.

(f)(7) As used in this subsection, the term "covered multifamily dwellings" means—

(A) buildings consisting of 4 or more units if such buildings have one or more elevators; and

(B) ground floor units in other buildings consisting of 4 or more units.

(f)(8) Nothing in this subchapter shall be construed to invalidate or limit any law of a State or political subdivision of a State, or other jurisdiction in which this subchapter shall be effective, that requires dwellings to be designed and constructed in a manner that affords handicapped persons greater access than is required by this subchapter.

(f)(9) Nothing in this subsection requires that a dwelling be made available to an individual whose tenancy would constitute a direct threat to the health or safety of other individuals or whose tenancy would result in substantial physical damage to the property of others.

SECTION 3607. Religious organization or private club exemption

(a) Nothing in this subchapter shall prohibit a religious organization, association, or society, or any nonprofit institution or organization operated, supervised or controlled by or in conjunction with a religious organization, association, or society, from limiting the sale, rental or occupancy of dwellings which it owns or operates for other than a commercial purpose to persons of the same religion, or from giving preference to such persons, unless membership in such religion is restricted on account of race, color, or national origin. Nor shall anything in this subchapter prohibit a private club not in fact open to the public, which as an incident to its primary purpose or purposes provides lodgings which it owns or operates for other than a commercial purpose, from limiting the rental or occupancy of such lodgings to its members or from giving preference to its members.

(b)(1) Nothing in this subchapter limits the applicability of any reasonable local, State, or Federal restrictions regarding the maximum number of occupants permitted to occupy a dwelling. Nor does any provision in this subchapter regarding familial status apply with respect to housing for older persons.

(b)(2) As used in this section, "housing for older persons" means housing—

(A) provided under any State or Federal program that the Secretary determines is specifically designed and operated to assist elderly persons (as defined in the State or Federal program); or

(B) intended for, and solely occupied by, persons 62 years of age or older; or

(C) intended and operated for occupancy by persons 55 years of age or older, and—

(i) at least 80 percent of the occupied units are occupied by at least one person who is 55 years of age or older;

(ii) the housing facility or community publishes and adheres to policies and procedures that demonstrate the intent required under this subparagraph; and

(iii) the housing facility or community complies with rules issued by the Secretary for verification of occupancy, which shall—

(I) provide for verification by reliable surveys and affidavits; and

(II) include examples of the types of policies and procedures relevant to a determination of compliance with the requirement of clause (ii). Such surveys and affidavits shall be admissible in administrative and judicial proceedings for the purposes of such verification.

(b)(3) Housing shall not fail to meet the requirements for housing for older persons by reason of:

(A) persons residing in such housing as of September 13, 1988, who do not meet the age requirements of subsections (2)(B) or (C): Provided, That new occupants of such housing meet the age requirements of subsections (2)(B) or (C); or

(B) unoccupied units: Provided, That such units are reserved for occupancy by persons who meet the age requirements of subsections (2)(B) or (C).

(b)(4) Nothing in this subchapter prohibits conduct against a person because such person has been convicted by any court of competent jurisdiction of the illegal manufacture or distribution of a controlled substance as defined in section 802 of title 21.

(b)(5)(A) A person shall not be held personally liable for monetary damages for a violation of this subchapter if such person reasonably relied, in good faith, on the application of the exemption under this subsection relating to housing for older persons.

(b)(5)(B) For the purposes of this paragraph, a person may only show good faith reliance on the application of the exemption by showing that—

(i) such person has no actual knowledge that the facility or community is not, or will not be, eligible for such exemption; and

(ii) the facility or community has stated formally, in writing, that the facility or community complies with the requirements for such exemption.

SECTION 3610. Administrative enforcement; preliminary matters

(a) Complaints and answers

(1)(A)(i) An aggrieved person may, not later than one year after an alleged discriminatory housing practice has occurred or terminated, file a complaint with the Secretary alleging such discriminatory housing practice. The Secretary, on the Secretary's own initiative, may also file such a complaint.

(1)(A)(ii) Such complaints shall be in writing and shall contain such information and be in such form as the Secretary requires.

(1)(A)(iii) The Secretary may also investigate housing practices to determine whether a complaint should be brought under this section.

(1)(B) Upon the filing of such a complaint—

(i) the Secretary shall serve notice upon the aggrieved person acknowledging such filing and advising the aggrieved person of the time limits and choice of forums provided under this subchapter;

(ii) the Secretary shall, not later than 10 days after such filing or the identification of an additional respondent under paragraph (2), serve on the respondent a notice identifying the alleged discriminatory housing practice and advising such respondent of the procedural rights and obligations of respondents under this subchapter, together with a copy of the original complaint;

(iii) each respondent may file, not later than 10 days after receipt of notice from the Secretary, an answer to such complaint; and

(iv) the Secretary shall make an investigation of the alleged discriminatory housing practice and complete such investigation within 100 days after the filing of the complaint (or, when the Secretary takes further action under subsection (f)(2) of this section with respect to a complaint, within 100 days after the commencement of such further action), unless it is impracticable to do so.

(1)(C) If the Secretary is unable to complete the investigation within 100 days after the filing of the complaint (or, when the Secretary takes further action under subsection (f)(2) of this section with respect to a complaint, within 100 days after the commencement of such further action), the Secretary shall notify the complainant and respondent in writing of the reasons for not doing so.

(1)(D) Complaints and answers shall be under oath or affirmation, and may be reasonably and fairly amended at any time.

(2)(A) A person who is not named as a respondent in a complaint, but who is identified as a respondent in the course of investigation, may be joined as an additional or substitute respondent upon written notice, under paragraph (1), to such person, from the Secretary.

(2)(B) Such notice, in addition to meeting the requirements of paragraph (1), shall explain the basis for the Secretary's belief that the person to whom the notice is addressed is properly joined as a respondent.

(b) Investigative report and conciliation

(1) During the period beginning with the filing of such complaint and ending with the filing of a charge or a dismissal by the Secretary, the Secretary shall, to the extent feasible, engage in conciliation with respect to such complaint.

(2) A conciliation agreement arising out of such conciliation shall be an agreement between the respondent and the complainant, and shall be subject to approval by the Secretary.

(3) A conciliation agreement may provide for binding arbitration of the dispute arising from the complaint. Any such arbitration that results from a conciliation agreement may award appropriate relief, including monetary relief.

(4) Each conciliation agreement shall be made public unless the complainant and respondent otherwise agree and the Secretary determines that disclosure is not required to further the purposes of this subchapter.

(5)(A) At the end of each investigation under this section, the Secretary shall prepare a final investigative report containing—

(i) the names and dates of contacts with witnesses;

(ii) a summary and the dates of correspondence and other contacts with the aggrieved person and the respondent;

(iii) a summary description of other pertinent records;

(iv) a summary of witness statements; and

(v) answers to interrogatories.

(5)(B) A final report under this paragraph may be amended if additional evidence is later discovered.

(c) Failure to comply with conciliation agreement

Whenever the Secretary has reasonable cause to believe that a respondent has breached a conciliation agreement, the Secretary shall refer the matter to the Attorney General with a recommendation that a civil action be filed under section 3614 of this title for the enforcement of such agreement.

(d) Prohibitions and requirements with respect to disclosure of information

(1) Nothing said or done in the course of conciliation under this subchapter may be made public or used as evidence in a subsequent proceeding under this subchapter without the written consent of the persons concerned.

(2) Notwithstanding paragraph (1), the Secretary shall make available to the aggrieved person and the respondent, at any time, upon request following completion of the Secretary's investigation, information derived from an investigation and any final investigative report relating to that investigation.

(e) Prompt judicial action

(1) If the Secretary concludes at any time following the filing of a complaint that prompt judicial action is necessary to carry out the purposes of this subchapter, the Secretary may authorize a civil action for appropriate temporary or preliminary relief pending final disposition of the complaint under this section. Upon receipt of such an authorization, the Attorney General shall promptly commence and maintain such an action. Any temporary restraining order or other order granting preliminary or temporary relief shall be issued in accordance with the Federal Rules of Civil Procedure. The commencement of a civil action under this subsection does not affect the initiation or continuation of administrative proceedings under this section and section 3612 of this title.

(2) Whenever the Secretary has reason to believe that a basis may exist for the commencement of proceedings against any respondent under sections 3614(a) and 3614(c) of this title or for proceedings by any governmental licensing or supervisory authorities, the Secretary shall transmit the information upon which such belief is based to the Attorney General, or to such authorities, as the case may be.

(f) Referral for State or local proceedings

(1) Whenever a complaint alleges a discriminatory housing practice—

   (A) within the jurisdiction of a State or local public agency; and

   (B) as to which such agency has been certified by the Secretary under this subsection; the Secretary shall refer such complaint to that certified agency before taking any action with respect to such complaint.

(2) Except with the consent of such certified agency, the Secretary, after that referral is made, shall take no further action with respect to such complaint unless—

(A) the certified agency has failed to commence proceedings with respect to the complaint before the end of the 30th day after the date of such referral;

(B) the certified agency, having so commenced such proceedings, fails to carry forward such proceedings with reasonable promptness; or

(C) the Secretary determines that the certified agency no longer qualifies for certification under this subsection with respect to the relevant jurisdiction.

(3)(A) The Secretary may certify an agency under this subsection only if the Secretary determines that—

(i) the substantive rights protected by such agency in the jurisdiction with respect to which certification is to be made;

(ii) the procedures followed by such agency;

(iii) the remedies available to such agency; and

(iv) the availability of judicial review of such agency's action; are substantially equivalent to those created by and under this subchapter.

(3)(B) Before making such certification, the Secretary shall take into account the current practices and past performance, if any, of such agency.

(4) During the period which begins on September 13, 1988, and ends 40 months after September 13, 1988, each agency certified (including an agency certified for interim referrals pursuant to 24 CFR 115.11, unless such agency is subsequently denied recognition under 24 CFR 115.7) for the purposes of this subchapter on the day before September 13, 1988, shall for the purposes of this subsection be considered certified under this subsection with respect to those matters for which such agency was certified on September 13, 1988. If the Secretary determines in an individual case that an agency has not been able to meet the certification requirements within this 40-month period due to exceptional circumstances, such as the infrequency of legislative sessions in that jurisdiction, the Secretary may extend such period by not more than 8 months.

(5) Not less frequently than every 5 years, the Secretary shall determine whether each agency certified under this subsection continues to qualify for certification. The Secretary shall take appropriate action with respect to any agency not so qualifying.

(g) Reasonable cause determination and effect

(1) The Secretary shall, within 100 days after the filing of the complaint (or, when the Secretary takes further action under subsection (f)(2) of this section with respect to a complaint, within 100 days after the commencement of such further action), determine based on the facts whether reasonable cause exists to believe that a discriminatory housing practice has occurred or is about to occur, unless it is impracticable to do so, or unless the Secretary has approved a conciliation agreement with respect to the complaint. If the Secretary is unable to make the determination within 100 days after the filing of the complaint (or, when the Secretary takes further action under subsection (f)(2) of this section with respect to a complaint, within 100 days after the commencement of such further action), the Secretary shall notify the complainant and respondent in writing of the reasons for not doing so.

(2)(A) If the Secretary determines that reasonable cause exists to believe that a discriminatory housing practice has occurred or is about to occur, the Secretary shall, except as provided in subparagraph (C), immediately issue a charge on behalf of the aggrieved person, for further proceedings under section 3612 of this title.

(2)(B) Such charge—

(i) shall consist of a short and plain statement of the facts upon which the Secretary has found reasonable cause to believe that a discriminatory housing practice has occurred or is about to occur;

(ii) shall be based on the final investigative report; and

(iii) need not be limited to the facts or grounds alleged in the complaint filed under subsection (a) of this section.

(2)(C) If the Secretary determines that the matter involves the legality of any State or local zoning or other land use law or ordinance, the Secretary shall immediately refer the matter to the Attorney General for appropriate action under section 3614 of this title, instead of issuing such charge.

(3) If the Secretary determines that no reasonable cause exists to believe that a discriminatory housing practice has occurred or is about to occur, the Secretary shall promptly dismiss the complaint. The Secretary shall make public disclosure of each such dismissal.

(4) The Secretary may not issue a charge under this section regarding an alleged discriminatory housing practice after the beginning of the trial of a civil action commenced by the aggrieved party under an Act of Congress or a State law, seeking relief with respect to that discriminatory housing practice.

(h) Service of copies of charge

After the Secretary issues a charge under this section, the Secretary shall cause a copy thereof, together with information as to how to make an election under section 3612(a) of this title and the effect of such an election, to be served—

(1) on each respondent named in such charge, together with a notice of opportunity for a hearing at a time and place specified in the notice, unless that election is made; and

(2) on each aggrieved person on whose behalf the complaint was filed.

SECTION 3613. Enforcement by private persons

(a) Civil action

(1)(A) An aggrieved person may commence a civil action in an appropriate United States district court or State court not later than 2 years after the occurrence or the termination of an alleged discriminatory housing practice, or the breach of a conciliation agreement entered into under this subchapter, whichever occurs last, to obtain appropriate relief with respect to such discriminatory housing practice or breach.

(1)(B) The computation of such 2-year period shall not include any time during which an administrative proceeding under this subchapter was pending with respect to a complaint or charge under this subchapter based upon such discriminatory housing practice. This subparagraph does not apply to actions arising from a breach of a conciliation agreement.

(2) An aggrieved person may commence a civil action under this subsection whether or not a complaint has been filed under section 3610(a) of this title and without regard to the status of any such complaint, but if the Secretary or a State or local agency has obtained a conciliation agreement with the consent of an aggrieved person, no action may be filed under this subsection by such aggrieved person with respect to the alleged discriminatory housing practice which forms the basis for such complaint except for the purpose of enforcing the terms of such an agreement.

(3) An aggrieved person may not commence a civil action under this subsection with respect to an alleged discriminatory housing practice which forms the basis of a charge issued by the Secretary if an administrative law judge has commenced a hearing on the record under this subchapter with respect to such charge.

(b) Appointment of attorney by court

Upon application by a person alleging a discriminatory housing practice or a person against whom such a practice is alleged, the court may—

(1) appoint an attorney for such person; or

(2) authorize the commencement or continuation of a civil action under subsection (a) of this section without the payment of fees, costs, or security, if in the opinion of the court such person is financially unable to bear the costs of such action.

(c) Relief which may be granted

(1) In a civil action under subsection (a) of this section, if the court finds that a discriminatory housing practice has occurred or is about to occur, the court may award to the plaintiff actual and punitive damages, and subject to subsection (d) of this section, may grant as relief, as the court deems appropriate, any permanent or temporary injunction, temporary restraining order, or other order (including an order enjoining the defendant from engaging in such practice or ordering such affirmative action as may be appropriate).

(2) In a civil action under subsection (a) of this section, the court, in its discretion, may allow the prevailing party, other than the United States, a reasonable attorney's fee and costs. The United States shall be liable for such fees and costs to the same extent as a private person.

(d) Effect on certain sales, encumbrances, and rentals

Relief granted under this section shall not affect any contract, sale, encumbrance, or lease consummated before the granting of such relief and involving a bona fide purchaser, encumbrancer, or tenant, without actual notice of the filing of a complaint with the Secretary or civil action under this subchapter.

(e) Intervention by Attorney General

Upon timely application, the Attorney General may intervene in such civil action, if the Attorney General certifies that the case is of general public importance. Upon such intervention the Attorney General may obtain such relief as would be available to the

Attorney General under section 3614(e) of this title in a civil action to which such section applies.

SECTION 3615. Effect on State laws

Nothing in this subchapter shall be construed to invalidate or limit any law of a State or political subdivision of a State, or of any other jurisdiction in which this subchapter shall be effective, that grants, guarantees, or protects the same rights as are granted by this subchapter; but any law of a State, a political subdivision, or other such jurisdiction that purports to require or permit any action that would be a discriminatory housing practice under this subchapter shall to that extent be invalid.

SECTION 3617. Interference, coercion, or intimidation

It shall be unlawful to coerce, intimidate, threaten, or interfere with any person in the exercise or enjoyment of, or on account of his having exercised or enjoyed, or on account of his having aided or encouraged any other person in the exercise or enjoyment of, any right granted or protected by section 3603, 3604, 3605, or 3606 of this title.

SUBCHAPTER II—PREVENTION OF INTIMIDATION

SECTION 3631. Violations; penalties

Whoever, whether or not acting under color of law, by force or threat of force willfully injuries, intimidates or interferes with, or attempts to injure, intimidate or interfere with—

(a) any person because of his race, color, religion, sex, handicap (as such term is defined in section 3602 of this title), familial status (as such term is defined in section 3602 of this title), or national origin and because he is or has been selling, purchasing, renting, financing, occupying, or contracting or negotiating for the sale, purchase, rental, financing or occupation of any dwelling, or applying for or participating in any service, organization, or facility relating to the business of selling or renting dwellings; or

(b) any person because he is or has been, or in order to intimidate such person or any other person or any class of persons from—

(1) participating, without discrimination on account of race, color, religion, sex, handicap (as such term is defined in section 3602 of this title), familial status (as such term is defined in section 3602 of this title), or national origin, in any of the activities, services, organizations or facilities described in subsection (a) of this section; or

(2) affording another person or class of persons opportunity or protection so to participate; or (c) any citizen because he is or has been, or in order to discourage such citizen or any other citizen from lawfully aiding or encouraging other persons to participate, without discrimination on account of race, color, religion, sex, handicap (as such term is defined in section 3602 of this title), familial status (as such term is defined in section 3602 of this title), or national origin, in any of the activities, services, organizations or facilities described in subsection (a) of this section, or participating lawfully in speech or peaceful assembly opposing any denial of the opportunity to so participate—shall be fined under title 18 or imprisoned not more than one year, or both; and if bodily injury results from the acts committed in violation of this section or if such acts include the use, attempted use, or threatened use of a dangerous weapon, explosives, or fire shall be fined under title 18 or imprisoned not more than ten years, or both; and if death results from the acts committed in violation of this section or if such acts include kidnapping or an attempt to kidnap, aggravated sexual abuse or an attempt to commit aggravated sexual abuse, or an attempt to kill, shall be fined under title 18 or imprisoned for any term of years or for life, or both.

GLOSSARY

Abandonment—The tenant's remedy of moving out of a rental unit that is uninhabitable and that the landlord has not repaired within a reasonable time after receiving notice of the defects from the tenant.

Act of God—Manifestation of the forces of nature which are unpredictable and difficult to anticipate, such as lightning and earthquakes.

Agent—One who represents another known as the principal.

Anticipatory Breach of Contract—A breach committed before the arrival of the actual time of required performance.

Appeal—A request to a higher court to review a lower court's decision in a lawsuit.

Arbitration—Using a neutral third person to resolve a dispute instead of going to court. Unless the parties have agreed otherwise, the parties must follow the arbitrator's decision.

Arbitrator—A neutral third person, agreed to by the parties to a dispute, who hears and decides the dispute. An arbitrator is not a judge, but the parties must follow the arbitrator's decision. The decision is said to be "binding" on the parties.

Arrears—Payments which are due but not yet paid.

Assignee—An assignee is a person to whom an assignment is made, also known as a grantee.

Assignment—An agreement between the original tenant and a new tenant by which the new tenant takes over the lease of a rental unit and becomes responsible to the landlord for everything that the original tenant was responsible for. The original tenant is still responsible to the landlord if the new tenant doesn't live up to the lease obligations.

Boilerplate—Refers to standard language found almost universally in certain documents.

Breach of Contract—The failure, without any legal excuse, to perform any promise which forms the whole or the part of a contract.

Breach of Duty—In a general sense, any violation or omission of a legal or moral duty.

Breach of Warranty—An infraction of an express or implied agreement as to the title, quality, content or condition of a thing which is sold.

Certificate of Occupancy—A document issued by local governmental authorities which certifies that a building conforms to local building code regulations.

Chattel—Any tangible, movable piece of personal property as opposed to real property.

Commission—Compensation for services performed which is based on a percentage of an agreed amount.

Common Area—In landlord-tenant law, refers to the area of the premises which is used by all tenants, e.g. hallways, elevators, etc.

Condominium—The individual ownership of a single unit in a multi-unit structure together with an interest in the common areas.

Consideration—Something of value exchanged between parties to a contract, which is a requirement of a valid contract.

Contract—A contract is an agreement between two or more persons which creates an obligation to do or not to do a particular thing.

Cooperative—Ownership of stock in a corporation which owns property that is subdivided into individual units.

Covenant—A covenant is an agreement or promise to do or not to do a particular thing, as to bind oneself in contract.

Credit Report—A credit report refers to the document from a credit reporting agency setting forth a credit rating and pertinent financial data concerning a person or a company, which is used in evaluating the applicant's financial stability. A credit report shows, for example, whether the person pays his or her bills on time, has delinquent or charged-off accounts, has been sued, and is subject to court judgments.

Credit Reporting Agency—A business that keeps records of people's credit histories, and that reports credit history information to prospective creditors, including landlords.

Default—Default is a failure to discharge a duty or do that which ought to be done.

Default Judgment—A judgment issued by the court, without a hearing, after the tenant has failed to file a response to the landlord's complaint.

Demurrer—A legal response that a tenant can file in an unlawful detainer lawsuit to test the legal sufficiency of the charges made in the landlord's complaint.

Discrimination in Rental Housing—As it relates to rental housing, discrimination occurs when a person is denied housing, is told that housing is not available when the housing is actually available at that time, providing housing under inferior terms, or is provided segregated housing, because of a person's race, color, national origin, ancestry, religion, sex, sexual preference, age, disability, whether the person is married, or whether there are children under the age of 18 in the person's household. Discrimination also can occur upon the refusal to make reasonable accommodation for a person with a disability.

Domicile—The one place designated as an individual's permanent home.

Duty—The obligation, to which the law will give recognition and effect, to conform to a particular standard of conduct toward another.

Escrow—The arrangement for holding instruments or money which is not to be released until certain specified conditions are met.

Escrow Account—A bank account into which a tenant deposits withheld rent, to be withdrawn only when the landlord has corrected uninhabitable conditions in the rental unit or when the tenant is ordered by a court to pay withheld rent to the landlord.

Eviction—A court-administered proceeding for removing a tenant from a rental unit because the tenant has violated the rental agreement or did not comply with a notice ending the tenancy, also called an "unlawful detainer" lawsuit.

Eviction Notice—A notice that the landlord serves on the tenant when the tenant has violated the lease or rental agreement, also known as "three-day notice." The three-day notice usually instructs the tenant to either leave the rental unit or comply with the lease or rental agreement, for example, by paying past-due rent, within the three-day period.

Excuse—A matter alleged to be a reason for relief or exemption from some duty or obligation.

Fair Housing Organizations—Organizations that help renters resolve housing discrimination problems.

Federal Stay—An order of a federal bankruptcy court that temporarily stops proceedings in a state court, including an eviction proceeding.

Fixture—Chattel which has become permanently and physically attached to real property, and which would not be easily removed.

Forcible Entry—The entry on real property, against the possessor's will, without legal authority.

Guest—A person who does not have the rights of a tenant, such as a person who stays in a transient hotel for fewer than seven days.

Habitable—A rental unit in which the conditions are safe, healthy and fit for occupancy, and that substantially complies with those building and safety code standards that materially affect tenants' health and safety is said to be "habitable."

Hostile Possession—The actual possession of real property without the permission of the legal owner, with a claim of implied ownership by the possessor.

Holding Deposit—A deposit that a tenant gives to a landlord to hold a rental unit until the tenant pays the first month's rent and the security deposit.

Implied Warranty of Habitability—A legal rule that requires landlords to maintain their rental units in a condition fit for human beings to live in. In addition, a rental unit must substantially comply with building and housing code standards that materially affect tenants' health and safety.

Impossibility—Impossibility is a defense to breach of contract and arises when performance is impossible due to the destruction of the subject matter of the contract or the death of a person necessary for performance.

Improvement—The development of land or structures to increase the property value.

Invitee—One who enters another's property by invitation.

Item of Information—Information in a credit report that causes a creditor to deny credit or take other adverse action against an applicant, such as refusing to rent a rental unit to the applicant.

Landlord—A business or person who owns a rental unit, and who rents or leases the rental unit to another person, called a tenant.

Lease—A rental agreement, usually in writing, that establishes all the terms of the agreement and that lasts for a predetermined length of time, e.g., six months or one year.

Legal Aid Organizations—Organizations that provide free legal advice, representation, and other legal services in noncriminal cases to economically disadvantaged persons.

Lockout—When a landlord locks a tenant out of the rental unit with the intent of terminating the tenancy. Lockouts, and all other self-help eviction remedies, are illegal.

Lodger—A person who lives in a room in a house where the owner lives. The owner can enter all areas occupied by the lodger, and has overall control of the house.

Mediation—A process in which a neutral third person meets with the parties to a dispute in order to assist them in formulating a voluntary solution to the dispute.

Mitigation of Damages—The requirement that a person damaged due to another's acts, such as a breach of contract, must act reasonably to avoid or limit their losses, or risk denial of recovery for damages which could have been avoided.

Motion to Quash Service of Summons—A legal response that a tenant can file in an unlawful detainer lawsuit if the tenant believes that the landlord did not properly serve the summons and complaint.

Negligence—A person's carelessness—i.e., failure to use ordinary or reasonable care—that results in injury to another person or damage to another person's property.

Nonfreehold Estate—A leasehold.

Novation—In an assignment situation, a novation is an agreement by the landlord, the original tenant, and the new tenant that makes the new tenant, rather than the original tenant, solely responsible to the landlord.

Nuisance—The disturbance of another's use of their property, rendering continued use uncomfortable or inconvenient.

Periodic Rental Agreement—An oral or written rental agreement that states the length of time between rent payments, e.g., a week or a month, but not the total number of weeks or months that the agreement will be in effect.

Prepaid Rental Listing Services—Businesses that sell lists of available rental units.

Quiet Enjoyment—The right of an owner or lessor to have unimpaired use and enjoyment out of the property.

Reformation—An equitable remedy which calls for the rewriting of a contract involving a mutual mistake or fraud.

Relief from Forfeiture—An order by a court in an unlawful de-tainer—i.e., eviction—lawsuit that allows the losing tenant to remain in the rental unit, based on the tenant's ability to pay all of the rent that is due, or to otherwise fully comply with the lease.

Rent Control Ordinances—Laws in some communities that limit or prohibit rent increases, or that limit the circumstances in which a tenant can be evicted.

Rent Withholding—The tenant's remedy of not paying some or all of the rent if the landlord does not fix defects that make the rental unit uninhab-itable within a reasonable time after the landlord receives notice of the de-fects from the tenant.

Rental Agreement—An oral or written agreement between a tenant and a landlord, made before the tenant moves in, which establishes the terms of the tenancy, such as the amount of the rent and when it is due.

Rental Application—A form that a landlord may ask a tenant to fill out prior to renting that requests information about the tenant, such as the ten-ant's address, telephone number, employment history, credit references, etc.

Rental Period—The length of time between rental payments; for exam-ple, a week or a month.

Rental Unit—An apartment, house, duplex, or condominium that a landlord rents to a tenant to live in.

Renter's Insurance—Insurance protecting the tenant against property losses, such as losses from theft or fire. This insurance usually also protects the tenant against liability for claims or lawsuits filed by the landlord or by others alleging that the tenant negligently injured another person or prop-erty.

Repair and Deduct Remedy—The tenant's remedy of deducting from future rent the amount necessary to repair defects covered by the implied warranty of habitability. The amount deducted cannot be more than one month's rent.

Rescission—The cancellation of a contract which returns the parties to the positions they were in before the contract was made.

Residential Hotel—A building containing six or more guest rooms or efficiency units which are rented for occupation or for sleeping purposes by guests, and which also are the primary residence of these guests.

Retaliation—An act by a landlord, such as raising a tenant's rent, seeking to evict a tenant, or otherwise punishing a tenant because the tenant has used the repair and deduct remedy or the rent withholding remedy, or has asserted other tenant rights.

Security Deposit—A deposit or a fee that the landlord requires the tenant to pay at the beginning of the tenancy to protect the landlord, for example, if the tenant moves out owing rent, or leaves the rental unit damaged or less clean than when the tenant moved in.

Service—Legal requirements and procedures that seek to assure that the person to whom a legal notice is directed actually receives it.

Sublease—A separate rental agreement between the original tenant and a new tenant to whom the original tenant rents all or part of the rental unit. The new tenant is called a subtenant. The agreement between the original tenant and the landlord remains in force, and the original tenant continues to be responsible for paying the rent to the landlord and for other tenant's obligations.

Subpoena—An order from the court that requires the recipient to appear as a witness or provide evidence in a court proceeding.

Tenancy—The tenant's exclusive right, created by a rental agreement between the landlord and the tenant, to use and possess the landlord's rental unit.

Tenant—A person who rents or leases a rental unit from a landlord. The tenant obtains the right to the exclusive use and possession of the rental unit during the lease or rental period.

Tenant Screening Service—A business that collects and sells information on tenants, such as whether they pay their rent on time and whether they have been defendants in unlawful detainer lawsuits.

Uninhabitable—A rental unit which has such serious problems or defects that the tenant's health or safety is affected is "uninhabitable." A rental unit may be uninhabitable if it is not fit for human beings to live in, or if it fails to substantially comply with building and safety code standards that materially affect tenants' health and safety.

Unlawful Detainer Lawsuit—A lawsuit that a landlord must file and win before he or she can evict a tenant, also called an "eviction" lawsuit.

U.S. Department of Housing and Urban Development—The federal agency that enforces the federal fair housing law, which prohibits discrimination based on sex, race, religion, national or ethnic origin, familial status, or mental handicap.

Waive—To sign a written document—a "waiver"—giving up a right, claim, privilege, etc. In order for a waiver to be effective, the person giving the waiver must do so knowingly, and must know the right, claim, privilege, etc. that he or she is giving up.

Warranty of Habitability—A warranty by a landlord that leased premises are without defects which would render the premises unusable.

Writ of Possession—A document issued by the court after the landlord wins an unlawful detainer lawsuit. The writ of possession is served on the tenant by the sheriff. The writ informs the tenant that the tenant must leave the rental unit within a certain number of days, or the sheriff will forcibly remove the tenant.

Zoning—The government regulation of land use.

BIBLIOGRAPHY
AND
ADDITIONAL READING

Black's Law Dictionary, Fifth Edition. St. Paul, MN: West Publishing Company, 1979.

Cornell University Legal Information Institute (Date Visited: August 1998) [http://www.law.cornell.edu].

Florida Statutes (Date Visited: August 1998) [http://www.leg.state.fl.us/citizen/documents/statutes/1997/ch0083.part02.htm].

The Occupational Safety and Health Administration (OSHA) (Date Visited: July 1998) [http://www.osha.gov].

U.S. Department of Housing and Urban Development (HUD) (Date Visited: July 1998) [http://www.hud.gov].

The U.S. Department of Housing and Urban Development Office of Fair Housing and Equal Opportunity (Date Visited: July 1998) [http://www.fairhousing.org].

The U.S. Department of Housing and Urban Development Office of Lead Hazard Control (Date Visited: July 1998)' [http://www.hud.gov/lea/leahome.html].

Zuckerman, Howard R., Disalvo, Joseph A. and Parker, Dennis D. *Fair Housing Litigation Handbook.* New York, NY: Wiley Law Publications, 1993.